Organizations and Identity

Key Themes in Organizational Communication

Organizations and Identity

Gregory S. Larson and Rebecca Gill

polity

First published in 2017 by Polity Press

Polity Press
65 Bridge Street
Cambridge CB2 1UR, UK

Polity Press
350 Main Street
Malden, MA 02148, USA

ISBN-13: 978-0-7456-5362-4 (hardback)
ISBN-13: 978-0-7456-5363-1 (paperback)

A catalogue record for this book is available from the British Library.

Typeset in 11 on 13pt Sabon by
Servis Filmsetting Ltd, Stockport, Cheshire
Printed and bound in the UK by Clays Ltd, St Ives PLC

The publisher has used its best endeavors to ensure that the URLs for external websites referred to in this book are correct and active at the time of going to press. However, the publisher has no responsibility for the websites and can make no guarantee that a site will remain live or that the content is or will remain appropriate.

Every effort has been made to trace all copyright holders, but if any have been inadvertently overlooked the publisher will be pleased to include any necessary credits in any subsequent reprint or edition.

For further information on Polity, visit our website:
politybooks.com

Contents

1

Introduction

In contemporary society, the self is an increasingly fashionable object of both public fascination and scholarly interest. Popular television shows like *The Biggest Loser* or *The Bachelor* explore how to become a better, more fulfilled person while at the same time self-help and advice books sell millions of copies. From many different voices, we hear the self framed as a site of "work" – something that can be improved for personal and even social betterment. For scholars, the self has similarly been seen as an object for scrutiny. In social science disciplines ranging from psychology to sociology to geography to communication to organization studies, scholarship related to identity has boomed in the past thirty years. The popularity of identity research likely results from growing interest in asking foundational questions relevant to all humans: "Who am I?" and "How should I act?" (Alvesson, Ashcraft & Thomas 2008). To be sure, addressing these fundamental questions has long been the focus of art, religion, education, politics and scholarship, and yet in contemporary times, the importance of these questions has deepened as traditional anchors of identity, such as church, family and work have undergone radical transformations. With all these changes taking place in an increasingly globalized society, answering the question "Who am I?" becomes both more difficult and more complex. At the same time that organizations continue to play a significant role in answering this question for most people, organizations and the implications for identity that accompany them are themselves in flux.

1

Introduction

In this initial chapter, we seek to situate studies of identity in organizational communication and organization studies within a larger, ongoing story about the self and organizations. The intent is not to provide a comprehensive history of the theoretical development of the concept of the self (see Holstein & Gubrium 2000; Rose 1998), but rather to position conversations about identity in organization studies within a larger historical and cultural framework. Fundamentally, this chapter addresses this question: Why is understanding identity important for understanding contemporary organizations and organizing processes? Answering this question requires moving beyond studies of particular organizations to examine some broad trends and historical developments in society, work and organizations that all contribute to the salience of identity as a construct for explaining organizing and organizations.

Rise of the Individual Self

The importance of identity in organization studies must be understood in the context of a world in which the individual is positioned as a key way of understanding, regulating and organizing society. In contemporary Western society, human beings are construed as individuals having unique selves. It is thus important in the beginning of our discussion to recognize the importance of individual identity in contemporary society as a recent social construction:

> For it is only at this historical moment, and in a limited and localized geographical space, that human being is understood in terms of individuals who are selves, each equipped with an inner domain, a "psychology," which is structured by the interaction between particular biographical experience and certain general laws or processes of the human animal. (Rose 1998, p. 23)

This conception of humans as individuals is shaped by both historical circumstance (i.e., changing political and economic systems) as well as political positioning by groups to shape knowledge (e.g.,

2

growth of psychology as a discipline). Nikolas Rose (1998) argues that "the ways in which humans 'give meaning to experience' have their own history" (p. 25). In other words, it is not a natural "truth" that we conceive of the human being as an individual self, but rather it is a construction of both historical circumstance and political maneuvering. In particular, the rise of the individual in contemporary society is inextricably linked to the growth of psychology and related disciples that have shaped our understanding along these lines.

Increased Possibilities for Narrating the Self in the Globalized World

British sociologist Anthony Giddens (1991) asserted that the conditions of late modernity (i.e., that we live in a world characterized by information exchange, globalization and fluidity) are what make identity a complex and important contemporary issue. Throughout much of human history, the narratives available to frame an individual identity have been rather limited. Telling the story "who am I?" was constrained by the few variations of knowledge and experience deemed "legitimate" at the time. Imagine a Chinese peasant 200 years ago. The options available for this person to frame her story were limited by rather fixed societal discourses related to class, gender and cultural traditions. In many ways, much of the story of self was already written for that peasant and her identity was likely rather stable. Compare this to modern times in a globalized world where people have access to many stories, many lifestyles. Through communication technologies and modern media, one can see how other people live, how they act and how they present themselves to others. These windows into the lives of others provide many more possibilities for defining the self. This time in history, more than any other, provides multiple opportunities for forming narratives of the self.

As the influences on and opportunities for framing identity have increased, the construction of the self has become a focal point in Western culture. Rather than viewing identity as singular, fixed

3

and coherent, the self is now more often conceived as multiple and, at times, even conflicted. Individuals must manage many "facets" of their selves – as an employee, team member, parent, spouse, citizen, volunteer, etc. (Tracy & Trethewey 2005). Sometimes all these facets fit together nicely, but at other times, they conflict and must be managed. For instance, contemporary families experience one key challenge in balancing work and family identities (Nippert-Eng 1996). For parents of young children, being both a "good parent" and a "good worker" often results in conflicts that must be negotiated, often on a daily basis. The management of multiple identities, as a discursive practice, thus becomes the primary identity challenge in modern society and in modern organizations (Cheney 1991; Kuhn & Nelson 2002; Larson & Pepper 2003).

With increased opportunities for narrating the self, people spend considerable time and energy forming, shaping and managing their identities – a process known as identity work (Alvesson et al. 2008; Sveningsson & Alvesson 2003). Identity work involves "forming, repairing, maintaining, strengthening or revising" who we are (Sveningsson & Alvesson 2003, p. 1165). As humans, we engage in this process all the time, sometimes conscious of it (active identity work) and, at other times, unaware of the ongoing process (passive identity work). Think, for instance, about two "texts" that most college students produce: a Facebook page and a resumé. Both are undoubtedly exercises in identity management, and yet they are also quite different. What you choose to reveal about yourself on Facebook often says more about how you want to appear to your friends. Alternatively, your resumé is probably quite different, likely recounting only your professional experiences and accomplishments. Both represent constructions of you, but differ based upon the audience. Both also demonstrate how we can do identity work in passive as well as active ways (Wieland 2010); you are more likely conscious of different things when you represent yourself in your resumé as opposed to on your Facebook page. This is just one example of how the construction of the self and the management of different aspects of identity becomes a key challenge in contemporary society.

4

Introduction

One way to view the centrality of identity in popular Western culture is to consider the modern consumer. To a significant extent, our economy is based on *identity consumption*. In a post-Fordist economy, one in which production has moved away from single products aimed at mass audiences to custom products aimed at increasingly smaller niche markets, the construction of self is also largely a consumer process. Choosing a particular product or brand over another, particularly for younger generations, is often as much of a statement about who you think you are (or are not) as it is about the particular need or utility of a certain item (Kendall, Gill & Cheney 2007). Advertisers undoubtedly encourage choices of products based upon lifestyle and identity. When, for example, did you last see an advertisement for Nike shoes that focused on the utility of the shoe rather than the image of the Nike athlete? Likewise, choosing an iPhone or a Galaxy likely says something about you and how you see yourself. Products not only have functions, but send and reflect messages about identity.

In addition to our personal lives, self-making has also become a focal point in work and organizations. As Tracy and Trethewey (2005) note, "identity is increasingly constituted by public, profit-driven, and institutionalized discourses" (p. 173) that generate pressure on people to become more organizationally profitable and efficient workers and managers. Management consultants, like Steven Covey (1989), offer strategies for shaping the self into something more successful. Covey recommends, for instance, that being proactive, managing oneself and taking time out for spiritual and fitness activities will help generate security, freedom and power. Our book therefore engages these ways in which the self is shaped by our overlapping and numerous interactions with organizations in our lives, particularly work organizations and as related to work more broadly.

Organizations, Interests and the Shaping of Identities

Although we have intimated that people have the ability to choose from many different possible identities, we would underscore that people are not completely free to choose any identity they want. The construction of the self is contested, as the choices for self-definition are invariably shaped and constrained by various interests. Many interests, some readily observable, others more difficult to see, have a stake in how we label, identify and position ourselves. In the past, these key interests included the family, the church and the state as providers of narratives for defining the self, and those narratives often overlapped. In contemporary times in the Western world, the family, the church and the state continue to exert considerable influence, but often those interests are less closely aligned. In addition, the modern corporation has arisen as a major force, perhaps the prevailing force, in shaping who we think we are.

Communication scholar Stanley Deetz (1992) argues that the modern corporation has become the dominant institution in Western society. In describing the "corporate colonization of the life world," Deetz argues that multinational corporations exert considerable influence on many aspects of daily life. Our food is often produced by large corporations and bought at corporate grocery stores. Our time is structured around the corporate work week. Our news and entertainment comes from outlets owned by multinational corporations. Our education system is designed to teach the skills necessary to make people good workers. For Deetz and others, the rise of the modern corporation is concerning because these institutions have considerable influence on our lives, yet they are largely closed to public scrutiny. Deetz argues that the interests of the corporation subtly subsume other interests, and eventually come to be seen as normal and natural. For example, it has become commonplace for public universities to talk about students as consumers, mimicking the language of market capitalism without careful reflection about how this may change the relationships between teachers and students (see McMillan & Cheney 1996).

For research on identity, the rise of the modern corporation and the corporate colonization of the life world suggest that we must pay close attention to those interests and institutions that have a stake in shaping identities and how individuals both consent and resist. Modern corporations, in particular, suggest narratives for identity formation that often dominate other narratives, and so it is corporations and other work narratives that become key shapers of identities. On the other hand, people are not simply beholden to the interests of corporations and they also resist and alter these narratives. This contested nature of identity in the modern world provides another compelling reason to study identity. As a result, some identity researchers, primarily from the critical tradition, have focused on explaining how some identities are regulated and resisted. The contested nature of identity is a theme throughout the remainder of this book, particularly in Chapter 5.

Diversity: Telling Alternative Stories

A final factor influencing the salience of identity research in organizational communication and organization studies over the past three decades is growing attention to diversity. With the rise of globalization and the increase in diversity in the workplace, some organization scholars have begun to question basic assumptions about how we make sense of organizational life and whose experiences are represented in organizational research and theory. Traditionally in organization studies, much of our understanding of organizations comes from the perspective of white, middle class males (Ashcraft & Allen 2003). Although that perspective deserves consideration, it is also the case that other perspectives deserve scholarly and practical attention, particularly because they help us to challenge, diversify and enhance our theoretical knowledge, as Allen (1996) demonstrated in her re-framing of socialization processes from a lens of feminist standpoint theory. Difference matters in the construction and communication of social identities, as well as in the development of scholarship that helps us to better understand the world around us (Allen 2011).

In organization studies, feminist scholars led the way in exploring the ways in which different aspects of social identity shape the experiences of women in the workplace. Broadly speaking, feminist scholars call attention to the ways in which social constructions of gender, as a central organizing facet of social identity, produce and interpret the experiences of organizational life for women and men, where organizations, in turn, shape and organize constructions and performances of gender (Acker 1990; Ashcraft 2013; Bruni, Gherardi & Poggio 2004; Buzzanell 1994). Rather than seeing organizational life as gender neutral, they explore how (hegemonic) masculinity is normalized into organizational practice and how this "others" women (and men who do not meet a particular masculine norm) in many organizational contexts. For example, Alexandra Murphy (1998) studied the experiences of flight attendants as they trained and worked at a major airline. The airline required women to maintain a certain weight and dress in organizationally approved ways. Murphy's research showed how masculinized managerial discourses related to the ways women looked, acted and dressed, but were also resisted by flight attendants. Gender, as key aspect of identity, emerges from feminist research as consequential for understanding the experiences and practices of organizational life.

Although scholarship on gender represents the most developed line of study related to organizations and diversity, feminist scholars have called for increased attention to other facets of diversity and sameness, such as those related to race, class, ethnicity, age, ability, religion and sexuality, which may all feature, to varying degrees, in organizational contexts and sense-making. Here, scholars continue to theorize the ways in which such differences may intersect – an idea known as "intersectionality." Intersectionality refers to "an analysis claiming that systems of race, economic class, gender, sexuality, ethnicity, nation and age form mutually constructing features of social organization" (Collins 1998, p. 278). For example, Patricia Parker (2005) argues that most of our research on leadership comes from the perspective of white, middle-class males. In her research on African American women in leadership positions, she is able to articulate a perspective that suggests that it is not enough to consider only race or only gender when trying to understand the experiences of these executives. Diversity and intersectionality are key areas of contemporary and future identity research and are covered in much more detail in Chapter 4 of this book.

Defining Identity

In the next chapter we will explore how definitions of identity differ based upon the perspective one takes. For the overall purposes of this book though, we draw from Tim Kuhn's framing of identity as "the conception of the self reflexively and discursively understood by the self" (Kuhn 2006, p. 1340). Kuhn's definition is informed by the work of Giddens, as well as Ulrich Beck and Richard Sennett, all who seek to understand the development of the individual in relation to changing and fluid institutions and structures, drawing particular attention to the rise in flexibility and risk taking at work. What we like about Kuhn's definition is four-fold. It: (a) begins with the concept of the "self," drawing attention to how subjectivity is understood as individual, and also materially enacted in comparison to "others"; (b) acknowledges that part of the process of constructing an identity is self-examination and "thinking back" on oneself (that is, being reflexive); and yet (c) places discourse and communication squarely in identity construction processes, where our sense of who we are is social and collective – it is influenced by the messages and interactions around us; and finally, (d) does not make claims about identity as "fixed" and immutable, but insinuates that self-making is always an ongoing process. This definition therefore allows us to conceive of one's sense of self as changing in particular contexts or over time, and yet nonetheless shaped by external and sometimes enduring influences. We will, of course, come back to this definition and other ways of thinking about identity in later chapters, but this gives you a first look at the approach to identity we are taking.

We want to note, therefore, that this book is about the relationship between organizations and self identity rather than a specific exploration of "organizational identity." Organizational identity research tends to focus on the collective identity, image and reputation of an organization (see Cheney & Christensen 2001). Although "organizational identity" is related to the construction of individual identity and discussed in this volume in relationship to forming and regulating identities, it is not the primary focus of this book. That said, we do include a section on organizational identity in Chapter 3.

Concluding Thoughts

This chapter began with the question: why is understanding identity important for understanding organizations? As the previous discussion illustrates, the popularity of identity scholarship in organizational studies is, at least to some extent, a product of historical conditions that exist outside of the boundaries of any specific organization (Alvesson, Ashcraft & Thomas 2008). This chapter explored some of these cultural, social and historical conditions that make the study of identity ripe for current and future scholarship.

There have been numerous books written about organizations and identity, so why choose this one? This book argues for a discursive approach to understanding the relationship between organizations and identity and claims that such an approach offers advantages for both understanding identity as well as understanding how identity matters in organizational life. Despite that organizational communication scholarship has often been overlooked in terms of its contribution to identity scholarship, we believe that a communication lens is necessary for understanding not just *what identity is*, but *why identity is crafted and experienced by different people in different ways*. Particularly in a globalized and information-rich world, we observe that much about work today involves being a member of certain networks; making choices about the kinds of education, training and expertise you want; learning about and deciding on opportunities quickly; and working with people from different backgrounds and cultures – all activities that involve the negotiation of identity and which are grounded in communication. This book is intended as a resource for scholarship and as a teaching tool for graduate and upper-division undergraduate students to facilitate more interest and inquiry into identity from a communication perspective. We hope, then, that this book helps point out what is missing in the literature by failing to attend to this important facet of identity research, and makes an argument for the consequentiality of discursive-oriented research for understanding identity and organizations.

Discussion Questions

1. What stories about organizations did you grow up with? You might remember parents or other adults talking at length about the organizations for which they worked, becoming identified at an early age with a particular sports team or perhaps you lived above a local small business and saw much of the comings-and-goings of life around that business. What was your sense about those organizations, and how do you think they have been influential in shaping your identity?
2. Think of a time when you were prompted to think specifically about your identity. You may have found yourself wondering "who am I?" after leaving or graduating from a job or school, encountering someone who seems to be the complete opposite of you, having a profound new experience or even missing an opportunity that really resonated with you. What was your experience with this? Who did you talk to (or not) about trying to figure yourself out? How did you go about it – perhaps conversations with good friends, writing in your journal, prayer or spiritual inquiry or even putting up a Facebook post? What reactions did you receive that were helpful, and why were they helpful?
3. What are the identity narratives that you use to articulate your own identity? What stories do you tell about yourself to different audiences, for instance when meeting someone at a party, on a first date or at a job interview?

4. How are the things you buy related to who you are? What is the last item (clothes, shoes, gear, etc.) you bought that might be an example of identity consumption? What do you think this item communicates to others about who you are?
5. Facebook, Twitter and other social media have become popular ways of communicating and interacting online, and much attention has been given to the benefits, as well as detriments, of creating an online presence. If you participate in social media, how do you represent yourself in various forums? What strategic choices do you make about what to reveal about yourself, and how?

2

Exploring Communicative Approaches to Identity and Organizations

What does it mean to study organizations and identity from a communicative perspective? No one clear approach emerges, but rather a collection of approaches and conceptual orientations. This chapter attempts to make sense of the large amount of research conducted on identity and organizations in the past twenty-five years by organizing it according to theoretical traditions. There have been numerous attempts to organize the literature over the years, so we here attempt to draw common themes from these past overviews. This leads us to review six meta-theoretical lenses for studying organizations and identity. None of these lenses is inherently better or worse, but rather each provides a different viewpoint from which to understand the commonalities and differences among perspectives. Once we have reviewed these meta-theoretical perspectives, we turn to the main purpose of this chapter: to articulate a broad *discursive approach* to understanding organizations and identity. Overall, two key questions guide our discussion: (1) What are the primary ways in which scholars have conceptualized the relationship between communication, organizations and identity? and (2) What is unique about a communicative or discursive perspective for understanding organizations and identity?

13

Meta-Theoretical Lenses for Understanding Identity and Organizations

The relationship between identity and organizations has been explored from a variety of theoretical traditions. These traditions have *epistemological* implications for how identity is conceptualized and *methodological* implications for how identity is studied. The intent of this section is not to provide a comprehensive overview of these meta-theoretical traditions (See Burrell & Morgan 1979; Deetz 1996; May & Mumby 2005; Putnam & Pacanowsky 1983), but rather to suggest how identity and the relationship between identity and organizations are conceptualized and studied from each of these traditions. Thus, we provide brief overviews of six common perspectives for studying organizations and identity: post-positivism, social constructionism, critical theory, rhetorical theory, postmodernism and feminist theory.

Post-Positivism

Post-positivism represents a theoretical frame that, while one of many relevant traditions today, served as the dominant lens for much early organizational communication research and to this day represents a leading approach in most US schools of management. At its core, post-positivism is based on the belief that through systematic observation and scientific methods, scholars can explain social phenomena. This tradition focuses on discovering cause-and-effect relationships among variables through the process of proposing a hypothesis and then attempting to falsify that hypothesis (Corman 2005). Drawn from the scientific method used in the natural sciences, the application of post-positivism in the social sciences most often proceeds methodologically through controlled experiments and surveys.

From the post-positivist perspective, identity may generally be conceived as the essential, or "empirical self" (Holstein & Gubrium 2000) – the self that exists based upon self-observations and reflections on the observations made by others. In this view, the self is viewed as an enduring set of traits, properties or beliefs that distinguishes one individual from the next. Furthermore, humans are understood to be self-conscious agents, a primary category of understanding (Holstein & Gubrium 2000). Although often conceived as possessing a psychological "truth," the self from this perspective is also often understood as influenced through communicative interaction. Although we could argue that there are few "true" post-positivists in organizational communication (Corman 2005), the most common application of a post-positivist approach in the study of organizations and identity comes from Social Identity Theory (SIT), which we discuss further in Chapter 3.

Social Construction

The social constructionist perspective is based upon the idea that language constructs our social reality. Rather than having a pre-existing reality that is out there waiting to be discovered (the post-positivist approach above), the social constructionist approach suggests that it is through use of symbols that we construct a meaningful world. From this perspective, communication is not simply a conduit through which messages are exchanged, but rather a productive, creative force in the creation of meaning. For example, think about the $20 bill that you might get out of an ATM machine before you go out with friends on a Friday night. The $20 bill has a physical/material reality that consists of the paper and ink that it is printed on, but (notwithstanding the significance of Harriet Tubman being selected for the front of the $20!, Calmes 2016) the physical/material elements of the $20 bill are not worth very much in and of themselves. Instead, it is the *symbolic value*, the socially agreed upon value of that currency that determines its significance and provides its worth, or its "reality" in negotiating social life, such as when buying a movie ticket (try discussing that next time you're seeing a movie with friends!). Particularly because of the debate over who "belongs" on US currency, we can see how symbols, like language, are consequential for constructing social meaning.

The social constructionist approach conceives of identity as a socially constructed interpretive "frame." That is, the self is created and understood through language use and related meaning construction, and this self then serves as a framework for interpreting and communicating with others going forward. Identities are therefore both created through communication and reflected in communication. From this perspective, we might think of identity as a story or narrative of the self that is constantly being told and retold (Giddens 1991). For instance, Holmer Nadesan (1996) showed how women service workers employed at a university reframed their low-status positions in the university system by articulating themselves as "mothers away from home" or "second mothers" (p. 73). This articulation of self, among other narrations, serves to establish a sense of self that influences how the women service workers see themselves, their identities.

For organizational scholars, a social constructionist perspective on identity points to the ways in which organizations, occupations and work itself all serve to symbolically shape meanings and produce discourses that influence individual identity construction. This approach suggests that we shape our identity by drawing upon various discourses that are fostered and endorsed by various social groups. These groups might include broad social categories like gender, race, class or other categories with which we identify, or more specific categories like a social group (perhaps a snowboarding club) or particular organization (are you a Mac or a PC?). The self exists in relationship to these groups, which helps to define identity by providing compelling stories, offering particular affordances for defining a positive sense of the self, or serving as a resource for identification (we see this in Edwards' (2011) distinction between who could call themselves a "googler" versus a "noogler," or person new to Google, in Google's early start-up days). Organizations, occupations and work all provide key discursive resources that people can use to construct their identities. Although individuals can accept or reject these discourses, it is important to recognize that identity is often shaped in some sort of conversation with such discourses. For example, Larson and Pepper (2003) found that when employees at an aerospace company were faced with significant organizational changes, they managed the impact of these changes for their identities by drawing upon the exalted values of the old organization in order to resist those changes. In doing this, the employees drew upon the (old) organizational values to also resist the (new) organizational values.

Overall, social constructionism remains a powerful lens for understanding identity and organizations. Research from this perspective shows communication as actively constructing identities, and in most cases, individuals are assumed to be purposeful in articulating their selves in the context of available, competing stories. On the other hand, a social construction approach is often critiqued for focusing too much on agency – or, the ability of individuals to actively construct and choose meanings and their identities – and not enough on the influence of organizations or other structures – or, the rules and resources provided by an organization or institution. The following perspective, the critical perspective, addresses this concern. You'll note in our overview of the critical perspective, as well as the other perspectives, the presence of social constructionism; social constructionism in many cases serves as the "base" on which these other perspectives are built.

Critical Approaches

The critical perspective on organizations attempts to explain the ways in which power is used in societal and organizational contexts to shape meanings and systematically distort communication (Deetz 1992). The goal of critical research is therefore to understand, expose and change inequities in organizational life, often through the promotion of discursive challenges from diverse or alternative interests and voices. Like social constructionists, critical scholars see the world as constructed through communication processes, yet they see these processes as fundamentally mediated by power. As Deetz (1995) states, "Once we understand that our world, our cultural life, is a social construction, we should know by whom and to what ends it was constructed in this way and have some choice in the matter" (p. 89). As such, critical scholars see a

17

world in which that which is believed to be normal and natural – "the way things are" – is really a social construction accomplished in unequal power relations. Belief systems or ideologies are constructed to serve and protect certain interests while at the same time silencing or distorting other perspectives or interests. Thus, the notion of *hegemonic ideology* refers to the ways in which people adopt a belief system as their own when that belief system does not really serve their interests (Mumby 1997). For instance, it is estimated that the "estate tax" (termed the "death tax" by its critics) affects roughly 2% of the estates in the United States, and yet a majority of the public supports repealing the tax (the estate tax is paid on estates worth $5,250,000 (IRS 2013) when those estates are handed down to descendants after the death of the primary owner). We can ask, though, why a majority of people prefer repealing a tax that affects only roughly 2% of the wealthiest Americans? While there is no simple answer, one theory about the unpopularity of the law is tied to deep-seated beliefs about fairness and the rights of people to pass their wealth along to whomever they choose (see Bowman 2009). Another explanation suggests that many Americans still believe the "Horatio Alger" myth, which suggests that those in the lowest income brackets can work their way into the top income brackets (see Waldman 2010). Despite the growing rarity of such social mobility in contemporary American society, this powerful narrative may influence people, regardless of their own anticipated estate value, to reject a tax on their "future" wealth. Both of these explanations for the unpopularity of the estate tax might be viewed as examples of belief systems that do not necessarily support the (financial) interests of the people who continue to hold these beliefs. Critical scholars would advocate uncovering and debating the underlying assumptions behind such beliefs.

A critical approach conceives of identity as a socially constructed site of struggle as multiple interests vie to shape or even "control" individual identities. From this perspective, identities are shifting and changing rather than fixed and stable (Deetz 1995), though some aspects of identity may be more enduring. In their research, Sveningsson and Alvesson (2003) told the story of "H," a manager

18

whose characterization of herself as "a farmer, a simple woman with 'both her feet on the ground'" (p. 1185), despite her in-flux role at work, represented a dimension of identity that is "less 'on the move' – being more stable or slow moving" (p. 1166). With this, we can see that rather than conceiving of the self as unitary or singular (i.e., one "thing"), the self is better understood as consisting of multiple, overlapping identities that "move" at different paces. From a critical perspective, these multiple identities are shaped and constructed socially, but in a world where certain interests have more power to shape identities than others. As a result, critical scholars talk about the self as produced through powerful socio-cultural discourses (Holmer Nadesan 2002; Holmer Nadesan & Trethewey 2001; Trethewey 1997; 1999). One example that might resonate with some readers is found in Eleff and Trethewey's (2006) research. Eleff and Trethewey discussed the pressure put on parents to throw perfect, boutique birthday parties for children. This pressure comes not from one source but from a conglomerate of sources, including parenting magazines, toy companies and party planners. In contrast to the social constructionist perspective that stresses the agency of individuals in shaping their identities, the critical perspective tends to frame the individual as more passive and so instead highlights the role of (powerful) institutions, cultures and organizations as creating and endorsing discourses that influence who we are.

For critical scholars, identity is the primary site for organizational control. Operating under the basic assumption that if you can shape someone's identity you can also shape her/his decisions and actions, organizations and institutions are seen as attempting to influence individual identities (more or less purposefully). Take the concept of "the professional," for instance. We use this term often, and it carries certain connotations such as the performance of white-collar work and the enactment of certain behaviors (Cheney & Ashcraft 2007). That is, if you see yourself as a professional you are also likely to try to shape your behavior to align with what is understood to be professional behavior; people self-discipline in ways that are consistent with how they see themselves – their identities. Alvesson (1994), for instance, described how individuals in advertising occupations adopted attitudes, dress and behaviors that they saw as consonant with being "in advertising." In this way, identity becomes a primary mechanism for control in the modern world and organizations play a large role in shaping identities. From a critical perspective, scholarship focuses on uncovering the ways in which organizations shape identities and the ways in which people discipline themselves *in the interests of organizations*. Identity is therefore understood as a site of struggle (Alvesson 2010) because multiple and often competing interests within a socio-historical context claim a stake in shaping individual and collective identities.

Rhetorical Approaches

This focus on the role that organizations may play in identity construction segues us into a discussion of the rhetorical approach to organizations. A rhetorical approach to studying organizations foregrounds the use of language for persuasion and identification. Long ago, Aristotle described rhetoric as the study of the "available means of persuasion" (1954) and this focus on persuasion continues as a major unifying focus of rhetorical approaches to organizations. Persuasion also remains a central feature in contemporary organizational life as seen most obviously in activities like in public relations, crisis management, advocacy, lobbying and marketing, but also in daily organizational activities such as socialization rituals, newsletters and meetings (Cheney 2005). Much of the communication that takes place within organizations and much of the external communication by organizations involves efforts at persuading various audiences. For example, BP's corporate communication in the aftermath of the 2010 Gulf Oil Spill continues to this day to be aimed at persuading residents of the Gulf coast, consumers, regulators and government officials that the efforts of BP in response to the oil spill were comprehensive, responsible and effective (see Wickman 2014).

While classical rhetorical theory centers on the study of persuasion, contemporary rhetorical theory links persuasion with identity. For Kenneth Burke (1973), the foundational scholar in this area, the rhetorical situation is about congregation and segregation, or the ways in which people make linkages and draw boundaries between themselves and other groups and organizations. Accordingly, "a great deal of persuasion is tied up with issues of identity" (Cheney 2005, p. 76), in that many of the persuasive efforts of institutions and organizations are designed to get people to connect with or see themselves as part of "groups, organizations, professions, classes, etc." (Cheney 2005, p. 76). For rhetorical-organizational scholars, then, the study of *identification* – or how people are persuaded to link themselves to others – is a major focus in understanding contemporary rhetoric in organizations. Many of the persuasive efforts of organizations are designed to foster identification in members in order to shape their decision-making (Tompkins & Cheney 1985). In a classic organizational study of the US Forest Service, Kaufman (1960) showed how the Forest Service persuaded rangers to highly identify with the organization through such practices as forestry education and moving rangers around frequently so that they would connect more with the Forest Service than with local communities. As a result, rangers saw themselves as one with the Forest Service. Kaufman notes that the Forest Ranger, hundreds of miles away from his [sic] nearest supervisor, would make decisions exactly as if his supervisor were right there, supervising his every move. The high-level of identification produced predictable, almost predetermined behavior from the rangers.

The rhetorical approach to studying organizations and identity does a nice job of highlighting the strategic ways that language is used to influence identities. On the other hand, this approach is often criticized from a critical perspective for a failure to pay enough attention to power and power imbalances. Communication scholar George Cheney (2005) responds to such criticisms by stating,

> I wish to argue here that the more traditional rhetorical concepts informing what I'd call a "rhetorical sensibility" are valuable above all for their recognition of how *discourse links individual persuasive choices with organizational resources*. That is to say, that a modified vocabulary and theoretical framework of rhetoric helps us strike to the

heart of questions about how broad discourses, as well as discreet messages, accomplish action such as the establishment and maintenance
of the authority of a "corporate actor." (p. 68, emphasis in original)

In Cheney's view, a rhetorical approach focuses on how language
is used to accomplish or create something (and here we still see
the presence of social constructionism!), including the construction and maintenance of power relations. Rhetoric thus becomes
a useful tool for exploring the exercise of power in shaping identities through persuasive communicative practices. It is also worth
noting, thus, that rhetorical scholars increasingly overlap with
critical scholars in their focus on examining power and inequality,
particularly in organizational contexts.

As envisioned by Raymie McKerrow (1989), for instance, the
"critical turn" in rhetoric "examines the dimensions of domination and freedom as these are exercised in a relativized world"
(p. 91), where critical rhetorical critiques must not only critique
domination in the service of fostering emancipation, but must
also continually revisit issues of power by critiquing "freedom" as
well (p. 91). Critical rhetorical scholars who overlap with critical
organizational scholars have examined, for instance, representations of success and labor, as in Dana Cloud's (1996) assessment
of the hegemony of Oprah Winfrey's "rags-to-riches" story.
More recently, Discenna's (2010) analysis of the 1995 graduate
student strike at Yale University demonstrated the role that social
movement organizing plays in constructing an identity around a
particular type of labor. Perhaps unsurprisingly, environmental
rhetoric scholars also quite often overlap with organizational
scholars in their focus on the role that corporations play in threat-
ening and/or enhancing the life of the communities around them.
Along these lines, Steve Schwarze (2003) offers a critique of inter-
organizational rhetoric in his examination of the irresponsibility
of mining company W.R. Grace regarding vermiculite mining
in Libby, Montana. Here, Schwarze demonstrates that the term
"corporate social responsibility" overlooks the role that other
agencies (such as local governments) may have in perpetuating
irresponsibility.

A Postmodern Perspective

The postmodern perspective (which aligns in some ways with *poststructuralism*) suggests a break from or challenge to the practices, beliefs and commitments of modernism. Modernism is most readily associated with the belief that rationality and science are the keys to human progress and liberation (Mumby 2013). The post-positivist perspective, discussed previously in this chapter, draws heavily from modernism in its faith in the scientific method as a means for uncovering the truth. Postmodernism, on the other hand, questions universal truths, grand narratives, predominant histories and what counts as "scientific progress." Postmodernism is better characterized by a rejection of the certainties of modernism than by any shared set of beliefs, assumptions or values. It is this deep suspicion and questioning of prevailing viewpoints and beliefs that best describes the postmodern perspective. That said, there are some common commitments and common rejections that organizational communication scholars use when taking up a postmodern perspective.

First, postmodern approaches suggest that discourse underlies all organizational processes (Taylor 2005). Like the social constructionist approach, postmodernists see social reality as interpreted and created through language or discourse, but they extend this idea in key ways. Although social constructionists might look for how shared meanings and experiences come to constitute the collective culture of an organization, postmodernists would instead focus on alternative meanings and perspectives that exist simultaneously with and in relationship to the prevailing organizational culture. Communication scholar Bryan Taylor uses the metaphor *intertextural* to describe this postmodern view of language and discourse (2005). This metaphor suggests that there are multiple discourses that influence the construction of social realities and identities, and that these discourses are interrelated. If you read David Boje's (1995) analysis of Disney as Tamara-Land, you'll see the way that postmodernists embrace multiple, overlapping and alternative narratives.

23

Second, postmodernists exhibit a common commitment to re-reading or re-interpreting common beliefs, meanings and discourses. The technique of "deconstruction" (Derrida 1976) consists of re-reading texts by thinking about alternative view points and meanings. For instance, Limerick (1987) re-storied the history of the settlement of the American West to include the experiences of Chinese immigrants working on the railroads. These viewpoints and others provide a much different "reality" of the history of the American West. Or take for instance, Calás and Smircich's (1991) deconstruction of foundational management texts such as Barnard's *The Functions of the Executive* and Peters and Waterman's *In Search of Excellence*. Here, Calás and Smircich envision such leadership texts as seduction manuals by considering the polysemous nature of management language and even noting the intertextual overlaps between these texts and sex manuals in circulation at the time. Clearly, deconstruction is a tool that supports the key postmodern tenet of questioning prevailing views and assumptions.

Perhaps more than the other approaches we've discussed, a postmodern perspective conceives of identities as multiple, contested and fragmented. This is a rejection of the empirical self of the modernist viewpoint – the self that is real, stable and enduring. For postmodernists, identities are largely produced through discourses, in that people often align their identities with dominant meanings. And yet, there are always competing discourses that challenge and alter the dominant discourses and this causes fragmentation to identities. For example, it is more common today for people to change careers. Although it is likely a myth that people change careers seven times in their lives (Bialik 2010), it has become both socially acceptable and at times necessary to reinvent oneself professionally (Alboher 2007). A related phenomenon illustrating the fragmented and decentered nature of postmodern identity, therefore, is the "slasher" – someone who can't describe what she or he does with a single word or phrase like "plumber." Instead, many people when asked to describe what they do answer something like one *New York Times* columnist does: "journalist/author/writing coach" (Alboher 2007).

24

Each slash represents another part of one's work or professional identity.

Like social constructionists, postmodernists see language as shaping identities, but they focus on the array of discourses available for shaping identities and thus present a less stable view of identity. Furthermore, for postmodern scholars, there is nothing "outside of the text" so the very experience of the self is structured through language (Taylor 2005). In other words, we understand who we are and who we might become in the context of language systems that enable and constrain the possibilities for narrating the self – we could not imagine ourselves being something that is not already "offered" in language. Moreover, some of these discourses are more powerful than others, and this is where identity and organization come together.

Organizations are critical to understanding the creation and regulation of identities from a postmodern perspective. Organizations provide and shape many of the discourses available for the construction of identity within an environment where the boundaries between the workplace and popular culture are blurring (Carlone & Taylor 1998), or even the boundaries between consumer and brand ambassador (Kendall, Gill & Cheney 2007). That is, even when we are not "at work," our identity is influenced by the consumer choices we make and the organizations with which we choose to align (what is communicated, for instance, by making Lilly Pulitzer or lululemon mainstays of your wardrobe?). Furthermore, changes in the contemporary character of the workplace have implications for identity. Many of today's organizations, described alternatively as post-bureaucratic or post-Fordist, have "flatter structures, decentralized decision-making systems, small economies of scale, 'niche' production, increasing commodification of everyday life; more insecure, unstable employment, and a blurring of distinction between work and life" (Mumby 2013, p. 363). It is likely an overstatement to say that we are in a purely postmodern era of work (Best & Kellner 1991) – as we noted in Chapter 1, Giddens (1991) and others would instead characterize today's era as late-modern – and yet the changes noted above highlight the fluidity that is part of much of modern work life today. Together, these changes (re)produce a postmodern sense of identity as fragmented, decentered and product or consumer-focused.

Feminist Approaches

A feminist perspective on organizations suggests that gender is a primary mechanism through which work is constituted and organized (Ashcraft & Mumby 2004). There are numerous feminist approaches that scholars take, and they are linked to varying commitments and foci (see Ashcraft 2005; Buzzanell 1994), but one commitment that tends to be shared across feminist approaches is that of addressing the exclusion of women's voices in the structure and practice of work. From this perspective, gender is not just another variable in organizations, but rather a fundamental part of how work is organized, professions are defined, power relations are enacted and social norms are constructed. In other words, gender is a "basic constitutive feature of organization" (Ashcraft & Mumby 2004, p. 96). For example, bureaucracy is an organizational form that is often touted as "gender neutral" in that it is based upon a set of rational rules and principles that apply to everyone regardless of gender. Yet, feminist scholars critique this view by pointing to the ways in which bureaucratic organizations privilege a career path that is traditionally male (Ferguson 1984), depend on cheap female labor (Witz & Savage 1992) and ultimately, (re)produce patriarchal power relations (Pringle 1989). Gender, in this way, is thus inherent in the very nature of bureaucracy. Feminist perspectives uncover such gendered constructions and inequities in organizations, but also look to promote alternative voices and transform organizational experiences and practices. Communication scholar Dennis Mumby (2013) characterizes feminism as a "discourse of empowerment" for its focus not just on uncovering and understanding the gendered constructions in organizations, but its goal to actively work to challenge and change inequities.

Important to note, however – and as we unpack more in Chapter 5 – is the "difference turn" in organizational communication that challenges the concept that gender may be studied in isolation from other social identities and instead advocates intersectional viewpoints. Intersectionality, as we noted in Chapter 1, recognizes the ways in which social identities are intertwined, where gender is performed or given meaning as it is intersected by, for instance, sexual orientation, class, religious affiliation or geographic background. What this means for communication scholars is that it becomes important to examine how communication works to construct individuals and groups as similar and/or different from each other through what are seen as the "differences that make a difference." As Brenda J. Allen (2011) argues, the ways in which people are positioned as different from others does not always "make a difference," or *matter* in terms of inequality, oppression and privilege. That is, just being different from others in a given situation does not in and of itself signal inequality (Collins, Gill & Mease 2012). Rather, intersectionality highlights how social identity is always constructed and enacted within particular contexts, for instance, where identifying as Jewish may be felt and interpreted differently when you attend a Catholic school during the week versus synagogue on the weekend.

Thus, although feminist and gendered organizational communication takes gender as a central starting point, many contemporary scholars have embraced intersectionality as a more meaningful way to understand difference and diversity in and around organizations. Ashcraft (2011) has argued along these lines that although "gender is a primary way in which social identity and relations of power are configured" (Ashcraft 2005, p. 153), we are no longer doing responsible scholarship when we study gender in isolation. That is, gender is always also intersectional. Like social constructionists, feminist scholars see identity as constructed through language, and like critical scholars, they see this construction as mediated by power. Yet, feminist organizational communication scholars also extend and challenge these other perspectives by investigating difference as a fundamental influence on the construction of identity.

In terms of the relationship between identity and organizations, organization scholars study how social identities are constructed by and through the work that people do, the historical assumptions that underpin professions and occupations and organizations themselves. That is, not only do we enact our intersectional identities with others when "in the workplace," but the organization of work itself guides who we think is appropriate for certain jobs, and how we attempt to shape ourselves to fit in with occupations and organizations. Think, for instance, about the images that many of us hold about what a doctor, nurse, engineer, mechanic or flight attendant "looks" like. These jobs and professions are illustrative not only of work that is deeply entwined with assumptions of social identity (e.g., gender, class, ethnicity), but, as Ashcraft (2013) articulates, demonstrate how some occupations are constructed, over time, for certain identities more than others. Ashcraft refers to this as the "glass slipper," where occupations represent an invisible but fairly stable structure that can be tried on – and which ultimately fits some bodies but not others. This is not to say that there is a natural, predictable link between people and the jobs they do, but that the ways that occupations have been constructed has created enduring assumptions about who should do what kind of work. In the case of occupations in the commercial airline industry, Ashcraft argues that more (white) men are pilots not because they are naturally "better" at piloting (and in fact, the early days of the airline industry highlighted women and femininity in commercial aviation to demonstrate the safety of flying, Ashcraft & Mumby 2004), but because the very concept of the job was designed around masculinity; hence, for some men, "the slipper fits" and they appear as naturally predispositioned for piloting work. Through examples like this, feminist communication scholars show the ways in which work, occupation and profession are inherently (re)constructed through gender.

Overall, the five perspectives we reviewed here, and summarize in Table 2.1, represent different ways of conceptualizing the relationship between communication, organizations and identity. Scholars operating from each of these perspectives have made significant contributions to the study of organizations and identity. It is also worth noting that although these perspectives are presented in isolation above, it is often productive and

Table 2.1 Theoretical perspectives on the relationship between organizations and identity

Theoretical Tradition	Conceives identity as ...	Role of Communication ...	Relationship between identity and organizations ...
Post-Positivism	Identity resides within the individual – identity refers to an essential, coherent, person that exists outside of language	Managers can use communication to shape identities, often through the process of identification	Identity/identification is an important variable in influencing organizational outcomes (e.g., decision-making) and improving organizational performance
Social Constructionism	Identity is constructed in interaction and demonstrated and maintained in the narratives we accept and reject	Identities are created through communicative interaction, where communication is at the core of identity formation	Organizations provide discourses/ meanings/resources that individuals draw upon to narrate their identities and make sense of experience
Critical	Identity is a site of struggle/control that is constructed and influenced by external forces	Influential discourses make certain identities possible and desirable; Discourses produce individuals as subject positions. Communication as a tool of resistance	Organizations shape the identities of workers for purposes of control. Workers engage organizations when staging resistance efforts
Rhetorical	Identities are formed and reformed through identification processes, where the self is linked to other entities (congregating & segregating)	Persuasive communication creates identifications which ultimately shape identities; persuasion and identity are inextricably intertwined	Organizations and institutions persuade workers to accept managerially approved identities
Postmodern (Post-structuralist)	Identities are fragmented, conflicted and changing because they are produced through multiple texts (inter-textual) where competing narratives vie for influence. Identity does not reside outside of discourse	Multiple voices, often in tension, influence the construction of identity. The experience of the self is structured through language	Organizations convey preferred ideologies for identity construction – workers undertake identity work to both consent and resist
Feminist	Constructions of difference and sameness, particularly around gender, are the primary means through which identities are organized and performed	Identity is accomplished and (re)produced through communication and Discourse, particularly in accordance with organizational and occupational Discourse. Discourse is used and summoned for (gendered) identity work	Organizations are a milieu to perform social identity and guide the organization of social identities along patterns of difference and sameness, advantage and disadvantage

illuminating to combine, either in part or in whole, the perspectives when conducting research. For developing scholars, the key is to be able to articulate your meta-theoretical commitments and understand how the choices that you make fit together into a coherent argument about the nature of communication, identity and organization. In this next section, we draw from these and other theoretical traditions to frame a broad *discursive approach* to understanding identity and organizations.

A Discursive Approach to Understanding Organizations and Identity

In this book, we argue that understanding organizations and identity from a discursive perspective is fundamentally different from understanding these concepts from other perspectives. Not only is this perspective different, but it is also consequential in that it has important implications for conceptualizing identity and understanding the subsequent implications for identity-related processes in other areas of organizational life. To be clear, it is not our intention to devalue or minimize the contribution to studies of identity and organizations from other perspectives, but rather to consolidate the contributions of communication approaches as something that helps scholars to understand identity and organizations in ways that bring to the surface new insights. In addition, it is worth noting that a discursive approach to organizations and identity is not the exclusive realm of communication scholars, but is rather shared by many organization scholars who approach the study of organizations and identity with commitments to the discursive turn in organization studies (discussed below). In this section, we attempt to answer the question "so what?" about this approach. What is unique and consequential about studying identity from a discursive perspective? To make this argument, we'll begin by examining the discursive turn in organization studies before articulating common principles of this perspective on the relationship between identity and organizations.

The Discursive Turn

The linguistic or discursive turn in organization studies is premised on the belief that language is the key empirical artifact available for studying social science (Alvesson & Karreman 2000). From this perspective, language is both available in that it is something that scholars can study, and also consequential in that it *does* something, accomplishes something. In the discursive approach, the inter-subjective nature of meaning (Berger & Luckman 1967) becomes a key area of focus in that the interactive nature of the communication process is seen as consequential (Sigman 1995). Overall, the linguistic turn represents a significant shift in understanding the nature of the social world:

> In sum, the linguistic turn is not simply about the privileging of language or discourse in understanding human behavior (though it is partly that). More fundamentally, it involves a reconfiguration of how we understand and explore our mediated relationship to the world and each other. By recognizing the linguistic character of all experience we can move beyond subjective or objective, discursive versus realist conceptions of human behavior to examine the intersubjective character of social reality – a reality in which both the discursive and material are inextricably entwined, but are by no means isomorphic or reducible to each other. (Mumby 2011, p. 1149)

The linguistic turn has continued to have great impact in the field of organizational communication and organizational studies, and it continues to evolve our understanding of organizations from fixed entities where communication could be predicted and controlled to constitutive sites of meaning, communication and interaction.

That said, and as communication scholars know intimately, many different definitions of communication are in circulation across scholarship and in popular understandings, and so we want to clarify our approach to communication here, particularly as it relates to discourse. The approach to identity that we advocate in this book is a discursive one, and yet we see discourse as both comprised of communication and distinct from the way that many people commonly conceive of communication (i.e., as transmission of information). Because of this, we see "discursive" as potentially a better term for highlighting the constitutive or generative role of communication; to connect to recent research framing the communicative constitution of organizations (Putnam & Nicotera 2009; Taylor & Van Every 2000); and as perhaps a better way to capture the broad ideologies and ways of knowing epitomized in macro-level understandings of discourse (discussed more below). Thus, we embrace the distinction that Ashcraft (2007) makes between discourse and communication: a discourse approach recognizes how language creates contexts that make certain things possible, where context is comprised of "a (loosely) affiliated set of metaphors, images, stories, statements, meanings and so forth that generate a particular and socially recognizable version of people, things, events"; and communication is "the basic human activity of struggling over discursive possibilities amid the material circumstances of everyday life" (p. 11). As we discuss next, and at a simplified level, Ashcraft's definition of discourse is akin to the "big-D" understanding of Discourse and her definition of communication is akin to "little-d" discourse. Aligning with this is therefore intentional on our part, as our vision of a discursive approach is intended to acknowledge communication/discourse while centering the significant influence of Discourse in everyday communication and identity construction. Because these terms are frequently used interchangeably, we also often use these terms broadly, though clarify distinctions when necessary.

With this in mind, a brief clarification of how we understand discourse is in order. Although the term *discourse* is widely used in organization studies, the uses and definitions of the term are highly varied and contested. In defining discourse, we follow Alvesson and Karreman (2000) in making a distinction between discourse (also known as little little-d discourse) and Discourse (also known as Big-D Discourse). Little-d discourse is associated at the most basic level with the idea that communication creates something, does something – an agentic view of communication. For example, according to Speech Act Theory (Searle 1985), the act of a teacher saying "Raise your hand before you speak" is not simply the transmission of information, but also has effects on the way that students act. Scholars studying little-d discourse focus on the ways in which conversations work together to construct joint meaning. This meaning is not simply the transfer of information from one person to others, but rather a collectively created intersubjectivity achieved through the communication process (Berger & Luckman 1967), where raising one's hand before one speaks becomes a sign of good participation and contribution. Conversations that occur in everyday organizational settings, such as interactions that might take place formally in a sales meeting or informally at lunch, create meanings around what we do and in doing so, (re)create both organizations and identities.

Although studies of little-d discourse assert the constitutive role of communication, this role is not something to assume but rather something to investigate. How is meaning constructed through communication processes? How are organizations constructed by the people involved in them? How are identities constructed in the day-to-day engagement? These questions suggest an important focus for researchers from a discursive perspective – that of the communicative processes and practices of meaning construction. The little-d discourse perspective ultimately does a nice job of focusing on the creative, constitutive role of communication.

In contrast to discourse, *Discourse* refers to "general and enduring systems for the formation and articulation of ideas in a historically situated time" (Fairhurst & Putnam 2004, p. 8). Often drawn from the work of twentieth-century French Philosopher Michel Foucault, Discourse references larger patterns of thinking, systems of thought or bodies of knowledge. Rather than existing at the local and emergent level like discourse, Discourses are broad and *a priori* in that they exist in wide-spread beliefs of a particular culture or society developed over time. In contemporary society an example of Discourse is "enterprise Discourse," or the idea that businesses and other organizations should operate according to market conditions that align to the wishes of the sovereign customer (du Gay 2004; du Gay & Salaman 1992). Put in lay terms, the "customer is always right." This idea exists apart from any particular individual or organization and is hugely influential in the ways in which organizations make choices about organizing. Evidence of the power of this discourse is seen in the ways in which non-business organizations, like hospitals (Miller & French 2016), arts institutes and universities (Urciuoli 2014) have been reorganizing themselves of late to reflect entrepreneurial values and pay more attention to their "customers." Big-D Discourses ultimately shape the meanings of what's considered normal and natural in a given culture.

The distinction between discourse and Discourse presents an important starting point for understanding the different ways in which discourse has been used, but further distinctions are necessary to capture the varied ways that scholars conceive of the relationship between discourse and organizations. Fairhurst and Putnam (2004) surface three orientations to discourse and its relationship to organizations in extant scholarship: object orientation, becoming orientation and grounded in action orientation. Various iterations of the *object orientation* conceive of the organization as existing prior to discourse, as providing a "container" in which discursive activity takes place, as existing separate from its creators and as an object with material constraints. The key question asked by scholars from this perspective is "What do we know about discourse within organizations?" (p. 9). Overall, this orientation privileges structure and treats the organization as existing separate from the discourse which takes place within it. For example, if you conducted a study broadly focused on determining how managers use language to inspire volunteers working with the American Red Cross, you may investigate the outcomes of meetings and interactions between managers and volunteers while in the workplace, as well as the organizational documents provided to volunteers like policy manuals and work descriptions.

The second orientation, the *becoming orientation*, focuses on how discourse creates organizations. The key question asked from this perspective is "What is organizing about discourse?" (p. 16). From this orientation, organizations are produced, maintained and transformed through language processes. Overall, this orientation privileges the agency of actors through the process of organizing (as a verb) rather than the structure of the organization (as a noun). From this orientation, your study of the American Red Cross might examine how the scrutiny of nonprofit involvement in certain disasters and politics (e.g., Attkisson 2010; Wallis 2012) has influenced how clients, policy makers and volunteers feel about the nonprofit, and how the organization (i.e., managerial decision-making) is shaped through these changing opinions.

The third orientation, the *grounded in action orientation*, seeks to balance the agency of actors to produce organizing through discourse, with the enduring features and unique identities of organizations. The key question from this perspective is "How is the 'organization' grounded in . . . the continuous flow of discursive conduct?" (p. 16). This orientation reflects a structuration perspective, which conceives of agency and structure, discourse and organization as mutually constitutive and influential. Here, your study of the American Red Cross might examine how an influx of volunteers in the age of internet activism, arguably seeking "boutique" and "personal experience" kinds of volunteering (Knight 2007), shapes the organization in such a way that it fundamentally changes what we "know" about the Red Cross; and vice-versa: how are the identities of these "new" kinds of volunteers then also shaped by the Red Cross? In sum, these distinctions that Fairhurst and Putnam (2004) make regarding the relationship of discourse and organization provide a useful framework to conceive of the different ways that language and language systems impact and/or create organizations and organizing.

Grant, Hardy, Oswick and Putnam (2004) indicate that the study of organizational discourse is a "plurivocal project," meaning that it borrows from numerous philosophies, approaches and methods. Similarly, the study of organizations and identity from a discursive perspective also draws from various epistemological and methodological approaches rather than one unified set of beliefs. What these approaches do have in common is the shared belief that studies that situate language, talk, narratives and/or Foucauldian notions of discourse (Ainsworth & Hardy 2004) are central for understanding the construction of the self. More specifically, in the following section we identify five principles of a discursive approach to studying the relationship between identity and organizations. Combined, these five principles establish an "ideal type" for a discursive approach to studying identity. In practice, though, most studies from this approach, including our own, do not address all of these principles, or combine them in various ways. Rather, we put forth these principles to comprise our argument about the important commitments of a discursive approach to identity in organizations in hopes of generating conversations about how this approach can best inform our understanding of identity.

Five Principles of a Discursive Approach to Identity and Organizations

A discursive approach to studying organizations centers on five overlapping principles: communication as constitutive, identities as discursively constructed and mediated, discourse/Discourse as interrelated, identity and organizations as mutually constituted and power as shaping organization and identity.

Communication as constitutive. A discursive approach to studying organizations and identity begins with a constitutive – or social constructionist – view of communication. As discussed previously, such an approach suggests that communication is consequential for creating social reality. Rather than seeing communication as only the transmission of information, the constitutive view sees communication as generative of meaning, of organization and of identity. Furthermore, a constitutive view of communication suggests that "meaning is not sent and received, but collaboratively produced, contested and negotiated" (Sigman 1995, p. 6). During the process of communicative interaction, something happens that is not attributable to the sum of the individual parts – *the process matters*.

At the organizational level, for example, organizations may be understood as a series of conversations that constitute the organization (Brummans, Cooren, Robichaud & Taylor 2014; Cooren, 2015; Putnam & Nicotera 2009). For example, a hospital exists as an organization because of the many daily conversations between doctors, nurses, patients, administrators and others – it does not exist on its own, that is, as an intractable "fact" of nature. While it may be tempting to think of organizations as entities apart from communication, this perspective suggests that they exist in the interactions between participants. If patients, doctors and nurses stop communicating, the hospital ceases to exist as a hospital. For sure, hospitals as organizations also have material things such as buildings, beds and MRI machines, and these material things influence communicative processes, but even these material things are made meaningful through communicative processes.

Management theorist Chester Barnard (1938) long ago suggested that the informal gives rise to the formal. That is, the building blocks of large organizations and institutions begin as informal conversations. For example, Facebook is a company with hundreds of millions of users, worth billions of dollars and with thousands of employees. As depicted in the movie *The Social Network*, however, Facebook arose from the informal conversations of Mark Zuckerberg and his college roommates at Harvard in 2004. The formal organization that we know as Facebook was created through thousands of conversations over time that eventually created rules, hierarchies, structures and ultimately the corporation. This suggests that to understand the ways in which organizations work, scholars need to pay attention to how language is used to create, maintain, change and dissolve organizations.

Identities as discursively constructed and mediated. A constitutive view of communication suggests that not only are organizations produced through communication, but also who we are is produced through communicative processes. That is, identities are socially constructed during communicative interaction and reflection. Moreover, as communication scholars are urging us to recognize, communicative processes are undeniably material (see, e.g., Aakhus, Ballard, Flanagin, Kuhn, Leonardi, Mease & Miller 2011), in that when communicating with others, we do so by interacting in some way (a physical event, even if in cyberspace) and through the "lived" experience of being in our bodies.

Thus, this approach does not deny that humans have physical/ material bodies, though it recognizes the generativity of the social in shaping and defining the self. Communication scholar Dennis Mumby (2011) argues that:

> ... culture and meaning do not exist in social actors' heads as cognitive structure ..., but rather get played out in the dynamics of everyday discourses, practices, rituals, and so forth. Discourses, then, are not to be studied to gain access to mental processes, but as formations of social phenomena. If meaning is somehow "inside the heads" of autonomous social actors, then organizational discourse studies are reduced to analyzing member discourses as manifestations of already formed meanings – a view that positions discourse as epiphenomenal to both meaning and culture, rather than as medium and outcome of the dynamics of meaning construction. (p. 1158)

Drawing on Mumby here, we can see that a discursive approach positions identities as continually constructed through communicative processes rather than as preformed in our (sub)consciousness and only reflected in, or transmitted through, communication channels. From this perspective, identities are constituted through shared frameworks for asking and making meaning out of the question "Who am I?" In this "non-essentialist" view (Fairhurst 2007) identities are not wholly stable, fixed or unitary, but rather are continually produced and reproduced in communicative processes.

As discussed previously in Chapter 1, a useful definition of identity that takes a constitutive view of communication comes from Kuhn, who defines identity as "the conception of the self reflexively and discursively understood by the self" (Kuhn 2006, p. 1340). Drawn from Giddens (1991), this definition positions identity as a sort of self narrative that is told and retold by the person. The *Merriam-Webster* dictionary defines reflexive as "directed or turned back on itself" and this provides a nice starting point to think about Kuhn's definition of identity. The self is constructed through communicative interaction and reflection back on that communication. For example, say you consider yourself to be a compassionate person. How did you develop this sense of self? That sense of self likely derives from a whole range of factors including cultural norms regarding compassion, your own experiences, others' comments about you and your reactions to and reflections on all of the above. If something happens that challenges this notion of the self, such as walking by a homeless man on the street without dropping any money into his cup, this likely causes you to reflect on your sense of self as a compassionate person in light of this experience. You might ask yourself, "Can I be a compassionate person if I just walked by this homeless person?" You may answer "yes," reasoning that there are better ways to help the homeless and that money dropped in a cup could be used for destructive means. You may also reason "no," and consider changing your actions, the kinds of conversations you have with your friends, or your choices about what you study and where you work. In this process you are reflecting back on what you have said and done, as well as others' reactions to those things, and making sense in regard to (your) previously constructed categories for defining who you are. This is a discursive process that constitutes identity.

In addition, when we speak, we do so from a position of identity that reinforces and/or alters our identity to ourselves and to others. Cooren (2015) argues that our communicative interactions, "must reaffirm, enact or confirm" an identity (p. 95). Identity is thus not just constructed in discursive reflection specifically about identity, but rather in the everyday mundane communicative interactions with which we engage. For example, say your mother asks you to "please, take out the trash," and you respond by saying "okay, Mom." When your mother makes that communicative request, it is done so from an identity position (as your mom) and your response reinforces that identity and her right to speak in a particular way while at the same time confirming your identity as a "son" or "daughter." This interaction confirms and reinforces to you both, as well as to anyone who heard this interaction, your identities and your relationships to one another. Now we can certainly imagine different interactions in this scenario, and these might then have different consequences for the communicative construction of identity.

Investigates the relationship between Discourse/discourse. A discursive approach to understanding identity and organizations also suggests that scholars must explore the relationship between discourse and Discourse. Rather than seeing these as separate, it is the relationship or the "translation" between discourse and Discourse that provides the most fertile ground for scholarly insight. Separating discourse and Discourse or focusing only on one and not the other obscures the co-constructed nature of talk and text. In other words, organizations and identities are best understood at the interplay between communication as creative and constitutive (talk) and the ideologies, cultural norms and social structures produced through and influencing communication (texts). Similar to the grounded in action orientation of Fairhurst and Putnam (2004), this framework suggests that communicative action, while creative, is also constrained by previous communicative constructions. For example, in constructing a syllabus for a class, professors have lots of choices about what to include or exclude and these choices will undoubtedly shape the style and organization of the class. On the other hand, these choices are also constrained by cultural and organizational norms such as the types of information a syllabus must contain, students' expectations of a familiar and recognizable document and appropriate methods for evaluating student work. In a similar way, both organizations and identities are produced and maintained at the intersection of discourse and Discourse. That is, although we hypothetically have *carte blanche* in constructing an identity, we are also influenced and guided in this by what we see around us as "available."

For understanding identity, this suggests balancing the view of individuals as agents in constructing their own identities and as acted upon by powerful discourses. In the identity literature, this distinction often gets framed in terms of *identity work* and *identity regulation* (Alvesson, Ashcraft & Thomas 2008; Alvesson & Willmott 2002) where identity work focuses on the agency (or "work") of the individual in creating her/his own identity and identity regulation focuses on the Discourses that shape or produce identities. In studying identity, however, there is a tendency for both theoretical and practical reasons to focus on either discourse or Discourse. This tendency can be said to stem from the scientific approaches that inform identity study – because some traditions have sought to examine the reality they see around them, they have leaned toward the study of discourse. On the other hand, traditions that have sought to understand broad, historical eras and epistemes (systems of knowledge that make conditions possible), have often foregrounded Discourse. And, because academic training fosters expertise that is grounded in one (or a set of related) traditions, scholarship tends to focus only on *either* discourse *or* Discourse. Methodological traditions support this bifurcation, encouraging scholars to adopt methods that address one but not the other. Ultimately, however, we contend that discourse and Discourse are mutually constituted (simultaneously) and must be understood in relationship to one another, because we can only fully recognize the implication of discourse in the context of Discourse, and the impact of Discourse by seeing how it shows up in discourse (more on this later). Many of our readers will recognize this more broadly as the fundamental mediation between structure and agency that is structuration theory (Giddens 1991).

Identity and organizations as mutually constituted. From a discursive perspective, not only are both identity and organization constituted through discourse, but also in relationship to each other. We would say, actually, that it is difficult to separate identity and organization. On the one hand, our identities are formed in the context of organizational influences. Corporations, schools, religious organizations and others all provide discourses with which to shape individual identities. For example, Phillip Tompkins (2005) discussed how NASA, during the Apollo era, had a strong organizational culture that shaped the values and identities of many NASA employees. On the other hand, organizations are created and shaped by the identities of the founders and participants. It is easy to see how some companies are shaped by the identities of their founders such as Walt Disney at Disney Corporation or Steve Jobs at Apple. Smith and Einsenberg (1987), for instance, addressed some of the issues that may arise when a company founder's image is at odds with company practice

41

in their study of labor organizing at Disney World. Here, the "employees as family" metaphor that Walt seemingly supported was belied by many organizational policies and practices. In addition, we can also note that occupations themselves are shaped by the (gendered, raced, classed and so forth) identities of those who populate those occupations (Ashcraft 2007; 2013). Because of this mutual influence, "it leaves very much open to doubt whether an individual identity can ever be fully abstracted from the organizational" (Taylor & Van Every 2000, p. 232).

As we have alluded to previously, corporations also play a large role in shaping identities today beyond just the workplace. Corporations shape popular culture and this then shapes individual and collective identities. The term the "culture industry" references the ways in which mass media produce products and lifestyles that support the dominant, capitalist economic system (Horkheimer & Adorno 1988). For example, companies like Nike and Adidas project a certain type of lifestyle image rather than sell the utility of their products. Consumers, especially young consumers, purchase the latest sneaker brands that they see celebrity athletes endorsing, thus embracing a particular lifestyle image. We see this, too, with brands that purport to escape this relationship – The Body Shop, Ben & Jerry's and Patagonia, for instance. Consumption of these seemingly "non-corporate" products also come with their own implications for identity. Popular culture produces lifestyle images in conjunction with organizations that serve as important discourses for the shaping of identity in contemporary culture (Kendall, Gill & Cheney 2007; Knight 2007).

Considers the role of power. Aligning with the critical perspective discussed previously, we also argue for the importance of understanding discursive processes as inherently mediated by power. This position is consistent with a view of discourse that attempts to interrogate the ways in which communication functions to construct and reconstruct (preferred) meanings. Moreover, this is why we insist on incorporating both discourse and Discourse in studying identity – because to exclude one angle may obscure the power dynamics in operation in the other, and the ways in which they are connected. That is, some agents, organizations, interests and institutions have more power to shape meanings than others, and "[i]n this sense, the linguistic turn tradition is intrinsically political to the degree that it recovers and examines the contested character of constitutive processes" (Mumby 2011, p. 1150). Given this contested nature of meaning, it makes sense that scholars from a communication perspective pay attention to the ways in which power influences the communicative constitution of both organization and identity.

Concluding Thoughts

In this chapter, we have addressed two questions important for understanding the relationship between identity, organizations and communication: (1) What are the primary ways in which scholars have conceptualized the relationship between communication, organizations and identity? and (2) What is unique about a discursive perspective for understanding organizations and identity? In addressing these questions, we have demonstrated how different meta-theoretical commitments shape the nature of how scholars understand these processes. Scholars working from each of the perspectives examined (post-positivism, social constructionism, critical theory, rhetorical theory, postmodernism and feminist theory) have made important contributions to how we understand the ways in which identities are formed and regulated. Furthermore, in this chapter, we described the foundation for a discursive approach to the study of organizations and identity. Such an approach, grounded in the five principles discussed previously, is at the heart of the remainder of this book as we explore the consequential contributions of this approach.

Discussion Questions

1. Which of the five perspectives on identity rings truest to how you view your own identity? Which perspective do you think would be most

useful for studying identity? Which of these perspectives are most compatible? Least compatible?

2. How does a discursive approach to identity differ from a more traditional psychological approach to identity?

3. What does it mean to say that identity is constituted through communication? What parts of your identity are easier to see as communicatively constructed? What parts of your identity are more difficult to see as communicatively constructed?

4. Try to think of a time when you might have navigated the distinction between discourse and Discourse in your own work or identity. This might be in relation to school, where you relied (even if unknowingly) on seemingly universal standards of essay writing and formatting to complete an assignment, or in relation to work, where you may have been asked to take on a new project and, although you had creative leeway, still sought to replicate industry standards or best practices.

5. Consider an organization for which you work or volunteer. What are the messages you receive about work expectations or policies? What do these messages and how they are framed suggest about how the organization conceives of itself as an object, in a process of becoming or as grounded in action? How do you think this shapes your everyday experience with the organization? What might change if the organization adopted a different orientation?

3

Forming and Managing Identities

In the early 2000s, the United States National Science Foundation (NSF) started a program called IGERT (Interdisciplinary Graduate Education Research Training) that was designed to educate the next generation of scientists. The NSF recognized that the big problems in science and society, like climate change, could not be solved within disciplinary silos, but rather needed scientists who could work with those in other disciplines. IGERT represented a concerted effort to fundamentally change the education of graduate students in the sciences.

At one IGERT program at a university in the western United States, Ph.D. students in biology, ecology, computer science and mathematics came together to begin their graduate education as interdisciplinary scientists. Early on in the program, one student, Ellen, confronted the same dilemma that her peers faced. The IGERT program was asking her to identify with the program and to create an identity as an interdisciplinary scientist. And yet, she was also expected to earn a degree in a specific department and her advisor in the Biology Department had expectations as to what it meant to be a biologist and expected her to "become a biologist." In other words, she confronted a conflict as to what her developing identity as a professional and a researcher should be and was pulled in sometimes overlapping and sometimes competing directions for her loyalty. She and other students wrestled with certain questions as they tried to work through their identities during their first years in the program. What is an interdisciplinary identity?

How does one get a job as an interdisciplinary scientist in a world where most jobs are offered through traditional departments? How does one develop the necessary disciplinary identity to earn a Ph.D. in an interdisciplinary program? Students struggled to narrate their developing identities as scholars and were forced to constantly negotiate who they were within several competing academic worlds.

The story of this IGERT student is a story that happens regularly in organizational life as identities are not fixed (e.g., "I'm a biologist!"), but rather are formed, contested, changed, negotiated and renegotiated (e.g., "I'm a biologist, but I'm working with a meteorologist and sociologist right now, and picking up quite a bit from them, so I guess I'm expanding my expertise ..."). This chapter explores a modern world in which people must engage in constant identity work to form and manage their identities. In particular, the management of multiple identities, as a discursive practice, constitutes the primary identity challenge in modern society and in modern organizations (Cheney 1991; Kuhn & Nelson 2002; Larson & Pepper 2003). This chapter first examines two tensions – (1) identities as stable or insecure and (2) people as agents of identity or identity as determined – that all explanations of identity formation must navigate, and then explores the ways in which people form and manage their identities within this world.

Forming Identities

Tensions in Framing and Understanding Identity Formation and Management

In the previous chapter, we discussed six different meta-theoretical orientations that influence how scholars conceive of identity. The question, "How are identities formed?" varies in some ways according to each of these different orientations. Instead of discussing how identities are formed from each of these perspectives though, it may be more useful to think about two tensions that all explanations of identity formation and management must negotiate. The first tension deals with whether identity is conceptualized as stable or insecure. The second tension deals with whether individuals have the agency to create their own identities or whether their identities are largely produced by things outside of their control like social environments, cultures or discourses. Together, these two orientations provide a useful way to understand the varied identity research that explores the forming and management of identities.

A tension-centered or "dialectical" framework for understanding identity formation and management draws from the widely discussed meta-theoretical dimensions of all theory. In a critique of Burrell and Morgan's (1979) paradigms for organizational research, Deetz (1996) suggested that organizational scholarship aligned on two axes: dissensus vs. consensus and local/emergent vs. elite/a priori. In a similar vein, Alvesson (2010) utilized roughly the same two axes as a way to understand identity research: insecurity/ambiguity/ fluidity vs. coherence/robustness/direction and individual doing identity construction vs. context providing direction for identity construction. We use these two tensions as a way to make sense of different ways of understanding how identities are formed and how they are managed from a discursive perspective.

The first tension positions identity as rather stable and secure on the one hand and ambiguous and insecure on the other. But rather
[MORE THAN / INTERPRETATION]
than viewing identity as either completely unstable, precarious and insecure or, alternatively, as fixed, essential and long-term, most theorists take some sort of a middle ground position, asserting that identities are multiple and contested while still maintaining some elements of stability and consistency (Alvesson 2010; Sveningsson & Alvesson 2003). That is, in contemporary society we live in a world with many identity possibilities that individuals must manage, but at the same time there are elements of our identities that are more stable and enduring. We can see how this might be the case, for instance, for someone who emigrates from their country – although she might continue to identify with her home country, she also begins to develop an identity rooted to the new place. Along with this, the way that her nationality is

viewed in the new country might be different; what it means to be French in France is different from what it means to be French in Australia. Alvesson (2010) would frame a situation like this as a meta-theoretical tension between "modernist (essentialist) and post-modernist (constructionist) understandings" (p. 197) of identity. Figure 3.1 illustrates this.

Insecurity, ambiguity, flexibility ⟷ Coherence, robustness, direction

Figure 3.1
Source: Adapted from Alvesson 2010, p. 209

The second tension deals with whether agency for constructing and managing identities resides in the individual or in the context. In other words, do individuals construct their own identities in any way they choose through their own identity work, or does context in the form of "discourse, structure, powerful agents, [and a] messy world" (Alvesson 2010, p. 209) shape individual identities? Scholarship diverges on this. Some scholars posit that individuals have significant agency to shape and manage their own identities while others conceive of agency as much less robust, where big-D Discourses largely shape and determine one's identity. As previously, with the axis that separated the theories focused on a unified, stable self versus a fragmented and unstable self, agency is best conceptualized on a continuum between individuals as determining identity versus context as determining identity (Alvesson 2010). An example for this tension can be found in relation to the popular fitness program CrossFit. Is the identity of a "crossfitter" determined and controlled by the program's image, advertising and philosophy, or does a crossfitter take up, reject or challenge the CrossFit discourse in her or his own, unique way? Most scholarship, while giving preference to one side of the continuum or the other, also recognizes that humans are not completely free to shape their identities in any possible way, but are also not completely controlled and predetermined either. This would mean that the crossfitter's identity is *both* shaped by the fitness program *and* constructed in a unique way by the crossfitter. Figure 3.2 illustrates this continuum.

Individual doing identity construction ←——————→ Context (discourse, structure, powerful agents, messy world) providing identity direction

Figure 3.2
Source: Adapted from Alvesson 2010, p. 209

To help place these tensions (insecurity/coherence and individual/context) in conversation with the different meta-theoretical positions discussed in the previous chapter, we mapped the meta-theoretical positions alongside the tensions (Figure 3.3). The positioning of these boxes should be thought of as relative rather than as definitive positions. In fact, as we created this figure and thought about different studies representing different perspectives, we continually shifted the boxes (and could probably still do so!). Nonetheless, we believe that this figure offers a good starting point for a discussion about how these meta-theoretical positions align with the two tensions that all researchers must consider, and that it usefully visualizes the communicative approaches to identity in relation to each other.

Given the positions we ascribed to these six communicative

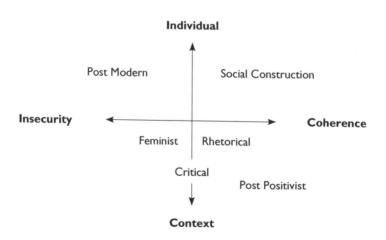

Figure 3.3 Meta-theoretical positions on organizations and identity

approaches, where would you map the discursive approach that we are suggesting in this book? Would it be in the individual agency/coherent quadrant? The identity-as-insecure/context-as-deterministic quadrant? It is more the case that scholarship that tilts toward any of these tensions could align with a discursive approach, but that some of the quadrants represent a discursive approach more readily than others. For instance, as the discursive approach takes communication as constitutive, it makes sense that discursive approaches to identity would view identity as becoming – as being (re)constructed by communicative process, and so lean more toward the notion of identity as insecure, flexible and fluid. Likewise, as the discursive approach sees identity as formed through a combination of contextual factors and individual agency, it would be positioned somewhere in the center of this tension, though would vary depending on the specific ways that a researcher embraced identity and framed it vis-à-vis their research. Although these tensions will move to the background in the sections below, they are worth keeping in mind as we discuss various perspectives on how identities are formed and managed. Our goal in the next section is to more deeply consider various explanations for the processes by which identities are formed and managed; the question you should consider here is "*okay, identity can be seen as fixed or fluid and shaped by self or shaped by other, but how does it actually get formed?*" To tackle this question, we next delve into three different ways of thinking about this: organizational identification, identity work and identity regulation.

Organizational Identification

In organization studies, the study of the formation of identities is linked to the concept of identification. We will explore specific definitions for identification in the following pages, but note for now that, broadly speaking, identification refers to the process of forming associations or linkages. Identification creates identities as we define ourselves through the linkages we make with others. As Cheney and Tompkins (1987) put it, "Today we thus find ourselves in the paradoxical position of declaring our essence, our uniqueness, in large part by expressing affiliation or identification with various organized groups, many being employing organizations" (p. 4). Think about the ways in which you define who you are by the groups you belong to: schools, teams, fraternities/ sororities, churches, families, workplaces and so forth. There are two primary schools in organization studies that have examined organizational identification: rhetorical approaches to identification and social identity theory.

Rhetorical Approaches to Organizational Identification

Some of the earliest organizational research to take seriously the communicative construction of identity comes from the merging of the rhetorical tradition and organizational research. In the mid-1960s, with newly minted Ph.D. in hand, organizational communication scholar Phillip K. Tompkins spent several summers at NASA's Marshall Space Flight Center in Huntsville, Alabama. The mid-1960s to early 1970s are considered the heyday of NASA as they comprised the "Apollo era" and the years leading up to the extraordinary accomplishment of putting a man on the moon. During the Apollo era, Tompkins noted a remarkable connection between those who worked for NASA and the organization itself, something he would later understand as organizational identification. Tompkins saw in the workers, and increasingly in himself, a sense that they were one with NASA. When writing about the consequences of this later, Tompkins (1993) illustrated this bond through what he called "automatic responsibility," in which NASA employees at the Marshall Space Flight Center automatically assumed responsibility for any problems they encountered regardless of whether or not they were officially in charge of that problem. In many large organizations, when problems arise that are not a particular worker's responsibility, she will either ignore the problem or, perhaps, make a note of it for someone else to deal with. At NASA though, organization members took ownership of any problems they found. This and related experiences at NASA shaped Tompkins' academic career as he searched for an explanation to explain this phenomenon.

Drawing from the work of rhetorical scholar Kenneth Burke, Tompkins and colleagues – especially George Cheney – developed a communicative understanding of how organizations and individuals become connected. In pointing to the connection between the individual and society, Burke (1984) stated, "The so-called 'I' is merely a unique combination of partially conflicting 'corporate we's'" (p. 264). From Burke's perspective, contemporary rhetoric is concerned with congregation (i.e., association) and segregation (i.e., division) and, in particular, how people are persuaded to move from feelings of "I" to feelings of "we."

Organizational identification, then, from a rhetorical perspective, is inherently about identity development and maintenance. Here, Cheney and Tompkins (1987) define *identity* as "what is commonly taken as representative of a person or group" and *identification* as "the appropriation of identity" (p. 5). Identification is thus the process of creating and maintaining the associations (and divisions) between individuals and others, which is understood as particularly formative in shaping the identity of the individual. And, although we often make identifications naturally, we can also be persuaded to form identifications. In contemporary society, organizations engage in persuasive efforts to encourage employees to identify with the organization.

That is, identities emerge in the appeals made by various individuals and organizations for affiliation and identification. For Cheney (1991), rhetoric – which can be understood at a basic level as the messages sent by an organization, or at a more complex level as the sense of being and identity constructed by and within an organization – enables individuals to form identifications and disidentifications with various groups and organizations. He states:

> All types of rhetoric involve appeal to the identifications, the associations, of human beings; organizational rhetoric involves the management of multiple identifications, multiple interests....."Rhetoric," then, is the arbitrator of "congregation" and "segregation"; it makes possible the moves from "I" to "we" and "we" to "I." (p. 20)

This explanation provides an explicitly communicative view of how identities are formed and managed as we engage and respond to appeals for association, often from powerful and attractive sources like employing organizations. This explanation also helps illuminate how we might define rhetoric. Although a basic definition may point to the messages sent by an organization as "rhetoric" (e.g., notices to employees, stories on the company website, advertising slogans), Cheney's discussion highlights rhetoric as intangible – the sense of being and identity persuasively constructed by and within an organization, though this may involve the tangible "texts" of an organization (DiSanza & Bullis 1999; Cheney 1983). In this, some appeals are going to be more alluring than others and thus, some identifications may be prioritized over others in particular contexts. Overall, this rhetorical perspective places much emphasis on the *process* of identification and how identifications are managed.

Cheney (1983) drew from Burke's theoretical framework of identification to study specific communication strategies that managers used to induce employees to form identifications with the organization. Looking at "house organs" like employee newsletters, Cheney found specific strategies and tactics used by management to encourage/increase identification. For example, the "assumed we" is the strategic use of "we" to rhetorically link the organization and the employee as one. Instead of making distinctions between members of the organization, such as between employees and managers, the use of "we" functions to mask differences and encourage the perception of oneness. Cheney argued the strategies and tactics used in these house organs were part of a larger "matrix" of persuasion strategies that organizations use to attempt to induce identification from employees. DiSanza and Bullis (1999) later extended this research by showing how employees responded to such identification inducements.

Central to this rhetorical understanding of identity is recognition that identification influences decision-making. Through communicative processes, like the creation and distribution of house organs mentioned in the previous example, or through socialization processes that workers experience, employees internalize the

53

organization's values and then draw on these values when they make decisions. The archetypical example of strong identification comes from Kaufman's previously discussed study of the US Forest Service (Tompkins & Cheney 1985). The forest ranger, through education and training in forestry as well as socialization processes, identified so strongly with the Forest Service that the ranger would make decisions exactly as if the supervisor were present, standing over him and observing every move.

The early research on identification in organizational communication studies emphasized decision-making as both an indicator and outcome of organizational identification (that is, decisions indicate the degree to which someone is identified and they are also the result of having become identified). Drawing from Herbert Simon's research on decision-making, Tompkins and Cheney (1985) defined *organizational identification* thusly: "A decision maker identifies with an organization when he or she desires to choose the alternative that best promotes the perceived interests of that organization" (p.194). Our identifications influence the decisions that we make and even the options we consider in decision-making processes. One way to examine this link between identity and decision-making is to consider "organizational identity."

Organizational Identity. The concept of organizational identity provides an avenue for understanding how organizations themselves construct an identity with which consumers and employees might then identify. As discussed by Cheney, Christensen and Dailey (2014), "an organization's identity corresponds to what is commonly used to *represent* the organization" (p. 698, emphasis in original), including key stereotypes and images. A fairly rich history of research on this topic has sought to understand organizational identity as an enduring quality of an organization and/or as a fluid social construction. A now-famous definition of organizational identity provided by Albert and Whetten (1985) suggests that "identity is the central, distinct, and enduring dimensions of an organization" (Cheney, Christensen & Dailey 2014, p. 697). In a different but related conceptualization, Cheney, Christensen and Dailey suggest a process orientation:

54

Ashforth and Mael (1996) define organizational identity as "unfolding and stylized narratives about the 'soul' or essence of the organization" (p. 21). From this perspective, organizations enact their identities through the stories they tell, directly or indirectly, about themselves, their past, their ambitions, and their perceptions of the environment. (p. 697)

As we can see, narrative is therefore essential to organizational identity in that it presents a coherent way of understanding and connecting to an organization. This point is underscored by ongoing discussions about the relationship between organizational identity and identification processes. In terms of the overlap between organizational identity and individual identity, when individuals identify with an organization, it is often the organization's identity with which they connect and associate.

For instance, think about the organizational identity of a well-known company like Apple Inc. What do you think of when you think of Apple? Perhaps you think about iPhones, iPads, and sleek silver laptops. Pushed further, you might think about Apple's distinctive style and the classy look of their products or their intuitive, easy-to-use interface. You also might think about Apple's logo – the apple-with-a-bite-out-of-it that was constructed very purposefully and carefully by Steve Jobs. If you think any of these things, you are noticing a carefully crafted image, or organizational identity, in which Apple invests millions of dollars to create and maintain. If you are an "Apple person" (e.g., committed to your iPhone) there is a good chance that you identify, at least somewhat, with the company and/or its image. Through this sense of identification, when some of us use our Apple products we are also hoping (at least secretly) that some of that positive image will rub off on us – i.e., "classy."

Furthermore, the organizational identity of Apple is also significant for its employees. Organizational identities not only provide an appealing target for identification for consumers, but for employees as well (Cheney & Christensen 2001). While there may be various internal meanings that employees associate with Apple, the broader public image is also potentially a significant influence on employees in forming identification with the company. If a woman says that she works for Apple and people react positively (e.g., "They make the best products – I love my iPhone"), this makes it likely that she will associate herself more closely with Apple and adopt part of Apple's positive image as her own. When this happens, one is likely to act and make decisions in ways that sustain and further this positive image for Apple.

Overall, organizational identity provides an important resource and target for organizational identification. Organizations invest considerable resources and talent in creating and sustaining positive, public organizational images, and consumers and employees often take note and associate with the images or "brands" they value. Accordingly, the disciplines of public relations and marketing focus largely on organizational identity. Although a thorough discussion of all the ways in which organizational identities are constructed and maintained is beyond the scope of this book, the image of the organization serves as an important discursive resource for forming identities and should be included as an important factor in shaping the identity of the individual.

Organizational Identification Questionnaire. Although Cheney and Tompkins envisioned organizational identification as a rhetorical process, some of the early research on identification used social scientific measurements to gauge correlations between organizational identification and organizational outcomes such as satisfaction or intent to leave. Cheney (1982; 1983b) developed a measure for assessing organizational identification called the Organizational Identification Questionnaire (OIQ) based upon three components of identification: membership, loyalty and similarity (p. 349). The OIQ proved useful in measuring identification levels in a wide array of circumstances including: with decision premises and decision-making (Tompkins & Cheney 1983; Bullis & Tompkins 1989), among mentors (Bullis & Bach 1989a), during turning points (Bullis & Bach 1989b), with professions (Russo 1998), with communication networks (Bullis & Bach 1991; Kuhn & Nelson 2002) and with multiple targets of identification (Barker & Tompkins 1994; Kuhn & Nelson 2002; Scott 1997; Scott et al. 1999; Scott & Timmerman 1999). For example,

Kuhn and Nelson (2002) compared centrality in communication networks with identification and found that people who communicated more with other members had stronger identification with more identity structures and those that communicated with fewer members had fewer identity structures with which they identified strongly. Overall, this body of research informs our understanding of the linkages between organizational identification and other organizational and communicative processes.

Despite the broad range of published research, the validity of the OIQ as a measure of identification as distinct from the related concept of commitment came under questioning (Sass & Canary 1991; Miller et al. 2000). The OIQ, as well as other attempts to develop measures of identification, has had difficulty establishing validity as distinct from measures of commitment, such as Mowday, Steers and Porter's (1979) Organizational Commitment Questionnaire (OCQ). Identification and commitment, while distinct, are highly interrelated concepts. Cheney and Tompkins (1987) refer to identification as the "substance" and commitment as the "form" of individual-organizational relationships. For these scholars, identification represents the process of forming identities through associations, where commitment is manifest in the "action" that results from this bond. For example, when one is highly identified with an organization, that identification is likely to manifest itself in commitment to the organization's work. On the other hand, there are times when one might be highly identified with an organization (i.e., one's alma mater), but not necessarily show commitment (e.g., donate money) or vice-versa. In retrospect, given the interrelatedness of identification and commitment, it's likely not surprising that scholars had such a hard time making distinctions in a survey questionnaire. The questioning of the distinctiveness of the OIQ as compared to the OCQ, in addition to the saturation of studies using the OIQ, led to decreased use of the instrument. In addition, organizational scholars from a discursive perspective turned their attention toward methods that explored the more communicative character of identification – an approach more consistent with Cheney's intended use of the OIQ as a tool to be used in conjunction with interview data (Miller et al. 2000).

Structuration Approach to Identification. An extension of this communication approach that attempts to conceptualize the relationship between identity and identification is Scott, Corman and Cheney's (1998) structurational model of identification. Drawing on structuration theory (Giddens 1984), the authors assert that *identity* represents the rules and resources that people draw upon to define who we are and shape how we act – the structure of identity. *Identification*, on the other hand, represents agency or the (re)construction of identity. Identification is thus framed here as a communicative, socially constructed process through which connections are made and, ultimately, through which identities are formed. This represents a uniquely communicative view of identification, as "the *process* of identification is conducted primarily with language, and the *product* of identification is expressed primarily with language" (Tompkins & Cheney 1987, p. 11). This approach further demonstrates the "duality of structure" (Giddens 1984), where identity as the product (structure) is shaped by, as well as shapes, identifications, and identification as the process (agency) is shaped by, as well as shapes, identity. Scott, Corman and Cheney's model conceptualizes identities as formed and managed through communicative processes of identification.

Social Identity Theory

Social identity theory (SIT) is a social-psychological theory that explains how identities are formed as individuals link themselves with others. Although there are many variations of SIT research, we would place most SIT work closer to the quadrant in figure 3.3 that emphasizes identity coherence and context. According to SIT, individuals have two parts of identity, a personal identity that is represented in personal characteristics, traits and beliefs, and a social identity that is represented in how people see themselves as part of various social groups or organizations (Tajfel & Turner 1986). For adherents to SIT and its closely related companion Social Classification Theory, answering the question "who am I?" involves classifying oneself as part of particular groups. Social groups include broad categorizations such as age, gender, race, sexual orientation and class, as well as more specific groups like a church, school, organization or work group. Through the process of "classification" individuals categorize themselves and others into specific groups, each category containing particular social meanings.

According to Ashforth and Mael (1989), social classification serves two functions. First, classification allows people to cognitively separate and arrange the social world into meaningful categories that allow them to make judgments about others based upon these categories. For example, a student categorized as a football player at a typical university might be thought of by other students as strong and athletic, but also as not very smart and not a good student. Obviously, as in this case, the assumptions made about those in particular categories are not necessarily correct. Nonetheless, the theory suggests that people do make assumptions based upon social categories and use these categories to assign attributes to and make judgments about individuals and, in this process, organize the social world into groups.

Second, in addition to providing a way to categorize others, classification also allows individuals to define themselves in relationship to the social world through the process of social identification. "Social identification is the perception of oneness with or belongingness to some human aggregate" (Ashforth & Mael 1989, p. 21). Through social identification, individuals link themselves to other social units or groups and in the process of doing so, provide at least a partial definition of the self. The groups that one identifies with serve as markers of one's identity and subsequently shape one's beliefs and actions. In other words, the theory suggests that one's beliefs and actions will coincide with the beliefs and preferred actions of a particular group. For example, for Greg to say that "I am a professor" provides him with an occupational identity that provides a meaningful category for understanding who he is, while at the same time providing guidance for how he should act. In addition, social identifications also serve to make distinctions, to define who Greg is not (e.g., an engineer, a dentist, a miner) and how he is not supposed to act. Social classification thus provides an important function in the process of identity formation.

For organizational scholars, SIT provides a way of explaining how organizations become part of who we are and how this process influences organizational outcomes, like commitment, loyalty and decision-making. Introduced to organizational scholars through Ashforth and Mael's (1989) influential article, SIT provides a way to see the organization as a (primary) category for identity construction. In contemporary society where many people spend considerable hours each week at work, organizations offer not just a paycheck, but also a way to define who you are. Illustrating this point, a recent advertising campaign by IBM ends with employees of the company stating, "I'm an IBMer." Similarly, people in many organizations might say "I'm a ... er" and in doing so they reveal their identification with the organization. For individuals this provides at least part of the basis for answering the question "Who am I?" and enhances self-esteem through this association with a positively viewed collective (Ashforth, Harrison & Corley 2008; Bardon, Josserand & Villeseche 2014).

For organizations, or more accurately, from the perspective of managers overseeing an organization, employee identification with the organization brings a host of organizational advantages. Past research links higher levels of organizational identification to a wide array of outcomes such as cooperative behavior (Dukerich, Golden & Shortell 2002), member support for the organization (Mael & Ashforth 1992) and turnover and intent to leave (Mael & Ashforth 1995) (for a review of more outcomes associated with organizational identification see Ashforth et al. 2008; Rikketa 2005). Because organizational identification is associated with such key organizational outcomes, this area of research has produced a lot of research from a management-oriented perspective.

Social identity theory represents a social psychological theory because it focuses heavily on explaining the cognitive processes that underlie social classification processes. As Ashforth et al. (2008) summarized, "The focus, then, is on cognition (I am A) and the high value one places on membership" (p. 328). Hogg and Terry (2000) explained the cognitive processes underlying social identity theory:

The responsiveness of social identity to immediate social contexts is a central feature of social identity theory – and self-categorization theory within it. The cognitive system, governed by uncertainty reduction and self-enhancement motives, matches social categories to properties of the social context and brings into active use (i.e., makes salient) that category rendering the social context and one's place within it subjectively most meaningful. Specifically, there is an interaction between category accessibility and category fit so that people draw on accessible categories and investigate how well they fit the social field. The category that best fits the field becomes salient in that context. (p. 125)

The underlying motivation behind these cognitive processes to identify with groups is to increase the positive valence about the self. In other words, people identify with groups they perceive as having high status as a way to give themselves high status. So in addition to cognition, identification "engages more than our cognitive self-categorization and our brains, it engages our hearts" (Harquail 1998, p. 225). That is, identifications are often emotional, as we often care deeply about the groups with which we identify. As any highly identified sports fan will tell you, when your team loses the big game, it hurts.

The focus of SIT on cognition can be critiqued from a discursive perspective for several reasons. First, a focus on cognition sometimes ignores the ways in which language and symbols shape our cognitions. Rather than seeing language as influencing and creating thoughts, in SIT "communication is viewed as a simple transmission of mental representation" (Fairhurst 2007, p. 50). Second, from the SIT perspective, identities are often assumed to be relatively stable (Alvesson, Ashcraft & Thomas 2008). While an organization might represent a relatively stable and coherent resource for identity in some contexts, in others the meaning of the organization may change across time and context. Particularly in contemporary society when the anchors for identity are changing, scholarship needs to account for the sometimes fleeting and fluctuating nature of our identifications and the ways we understand those identifications. Social identities themselves are socially constructed and understood, and social categories can have multiple meanings, even to the same people. Third and related, SIT's focus on cognition underemphasizes the multiple identities, the "concurrent and conflicting self-images" (Alvesson et al. 2008, p. 14) that are more readily engaged in discursive approaches to identity. Although more recent research on SIT has begun to address this limitation, a discursive perspective with a focus on the many available discourses for defining the self may be more suited to exploring these multiple identities.

Although SIT has traditionally focused on cognitive processes, some SIT research does focus on communication. Communication scholar Craig Scott (2007) illustrated that organizational communication scholars, as well as some management scholars, have begun exploring the role of communication processes in SIT. Scott (2007) pointed to five areas of overlap between communication research and SIT, involving: "dual/multiple identifications, computer-mediated communication and virtual work related to identification, relationally focused work identities, organizational-level identities, and disidentification and related forms" (p. 123). In the area of dual/multiple identification, Scott's own research provides examples of the integration of communication studies into SIT. For example, Scott and Stephens (2009) examined how communication with different persons influenced identification levels with various targets (conceptualized largely according to SIT) such as the organization, the nonprofit community and the performing arts. This research showed the situated and fluid nature of identification as identification levels changed alongside communicative actions with others. Through this, we can thus see some of the potential to link SIT with communication processes.

Overall, the organizational identification approach, particularly using SIT, has produced the bulk of identity-related research in organization studies to this point. As discussed previously, the rhetorical approach to identification is notable in that it represents an early attempt in organization studies to conceptualize identification and identity as communicatively constructed. On the other hand, the organizational identification approach, both from SIT and rhetorical approaches, has been critiqued for having a "thin" conceptualization of identity that is mostly about association and that assumes the significance of organizational identification as a central identity concern (Sveningsson & Alvesson 2003, p. 1165). In the following section, we examine approaches to identity that focus on the discursive identity work in which individuals engage when forming and managing their identities.

Identity Work

In comparison with organizational identification research that focuses on the connections and associations people make between organizations and their selves, the focus in identity work research shifts to the wider variety of ways in which personal identities are formed through symbolic processes. *Identity work* is often addressed by researchers broadly influenced by the discursive turn in organization studies who embrace the discursive process of identity formation and management. Research in this vein tends to approach the formation and management of identity from the perspective of the individual's ability (or, agency) to shape and manage her/his own identity. In other words, the individual engages in identity work and, while not free to shape an identity in any way desired, possesses considerable ability to form and manage an identity. One of the first recognized definitions of identity work comes from Sveningsson and Alvesson (2003):

> The concept *identity work* refers to people being engaged in forming, repairing, maintaining, strengthening or revising the constructions that are productive of a sense of coherence and distinctiveness. Identity work may either, in complex and fragmented contexts, be more or less continuously on-going or, in contexts high on stability, be a theme of engagement during crises or transitions. (p. 1165, emphasis in original)

Expanding from this definition, identity work is conceived as symbolic activity of the individual in which identity is continually produced and reproduced through communicative processes as individuals make sense of the social world around them and communicatively construct an ongoing identity narrative.

Although the focus of identity work is often individual identity and the narratives individuals form, such narratives are shaped through the feedback we receive from others that confirms or disconfirms our identity narratives. In this way, the social aspect of identity formation and management comes to the fore. For many scholars of identity work, personal and social identities are inherently connected in that "the self cannot be understood outside of the social because the self is inherently reflexive" (Wieland 2010, p. 506). In constructing a self-identity through identity work processes, people think back to how others see them and how others talk about them, and include this in their meaning-making of the self. In addition, through language we not only construct our own identities, but also influence how those around us frame their own identity narratives (Ainsworth & Hardy 2004). Adib and Guerrier (2003) argue that:

> Identity construction is both relational and contextual. It is relational in the sense that identity construction engages in Othering, a process which assumes a relationship of one identity to another. Identity construction is contextual in that the context in which this process occurs shapes the meanings, expectations and roles that particular identities carry. (p. 415)

Although many identity researchers implicitly include the social as part of individual identity work, some identity work scholars argue for a more explicit distinction between personal and social identities (Watson 2008; Wieland 2010). For these scholars, during identity work we may work on an "external" identity, which we portray to others, as well as an "internal" identity that we construct for ourselves (Watson 2008, p. 127).

The Substance of Identity Work

A discussion of identity work prompts questions regarding the resources that people use when "working" their identities. From a discursive perspective, the primary substance of identity work is discourse. As discussed previously, there are numerous ways to frame discourse narrowly, as in everyday conversations and stories, or more broadly, as in enduring Discourses that shape

Forming and Managing Identities

our worldviews. In defining identity work, Alvesson et al. (2008) suggest the term "cultural resources":

Identity work is prompted by social interaction that raises questions of "who am I?" and "who are we?" In attempting to answer these questions, an individual crafts a self-narrative by drawing on cultural resources as well as memories and desires to reproduce or transform their sense of self. (p. 15)

Whether framed as cultural resources or discourses, identity work scholarship conceptualizes the substance of identity as the socially and communicatively constructed meanings that shape (and are shaped by) our narratives of self. In addition, identity work scholars see individuals as active participants in accepting and rejecting the possible discourses that are available for identity formation.

We argue that from a discursive identity perspective, a useful way of framing what individuals draw upon when forming and managing their identities is the concept of *discursive resources.* Discursive resources function as the building blocks for identity, the substance from which people imagine various possible identities and form the narrative they do for themselves. According to Kuhn (2006), discursive resources are "concepts, expressions, or other linguistic devices that, when deployed in talk, present explanations for past and/or future activity that guide interactants' interpretation of experience while molding individual and collective action" (p. 1341). There are many potential discursive resources that individuals might draw upon when trying to shape identity narratives, including discourses that exist outside the boundaries of the organization like gender, race, sexuality, lifestyle and place. For example, Jorgenson (2002) explored how female engineers drew upon some possible discursive resources and rejected others during interviews about their careers. The participants in her study embraced discourses that constructed their professional identities as career-driven, qualified engineers who could do the sort of technical, mathematical work that relatively few people are capable of doing. They resisted the framing of their professional identities as "female engineers" because that framing represented a more marginalized account of their professional identities. Through positioning certain discourses as relevant or irrelevant to their professional identities in particular contexts, these engineers actively constructed their own professional identities.

At the same time that there are many discursive resources to draw upon during identity work, the meanings of discursive resources, themselves, are not static or fixed. From a discursive perspective, meanings are constantly being constructed and reconstructed through communicative processes. In addition, the meanings of discursive resources are political in that certain groups have a stake in seeing that one particular meaning emerges for a particular discursive resource rather than another. Turner and Norwood (2013), for instance, discuss how breastfeeding mothers work to construct a "good working mother" identity in the context of powerful professional Discourses that separate work and personal lives. While constrained in some ways, the women in this study also practiced "unbounded motherhood" through their integration of the historically separate Discourses of good worker and good mother. They rejected Discourses that suggested that the good working mother is a lesser identity and practiced mothering behaviors like breastfeeding in ways that provided the opportunities to make such practices routine. This study shows how discursive resources themselves can be shaped by the identity work of participants.

Despite that – or because – Discourse and discursive resources serve as the focal points for much research on identity work, scholars have also suggested that we need to consider "embodied practices" and "material and institutional arrangements" as part of the substance of identity work (Alvesson et al. 2008, p.19). For instance, Meisenbach (2008) found that the material success of fundraisers was a key factor in the construction of their occupational identities. Trethewey (1999) studied the materiality of women's bodies as constructed and disciplined in a professional, organizational setting. Their professional identities were shaped, in a significant way, by their female bodies. Finally, Barley and Kunda (2001), in a call to all organizational scholars, suggested that we need to pay closer attention to the things people actually do at work. As such, the activities and practices that individuals engage in while working also help to define who they are. From a discursive identity perspective, a key challenge is to explore the relationship between materiality, embodied practice and discourse.

Occupational Identity. One key discursive resource available for identity formation in contemporary society is occupational identity. Occupational identity refers to the collectively constructed image of an occupation that, as a theoretical construct, shifts focus away from the organization as a site of identity construction to the patterned practices and expectations of occupations (see Ashcraft 2013 for an overview and history of scholarship on occupations and professions). As Ashcraft (2013) explains, occupational identity "answers the question 'Who are we?' by way of what we do rather than where we do it" (p. 13). Importantly, a focus on occupational identity challenges the object orientation to organizations (as discussed in Chapter 2) that tethers identity construction to the container of an organization. Instead, occupational identity recognizes that work-related identity is constructed "in families, educational institutions, labor and professional associations, popular culture," as well as in relation to formal organizations (p. 13). Thus in many ways, occupational identity underlies much of what we discuss in this book.

In studying the occupations of pilot and flight attendant, for instance, Ashcraft demonstrates how these occupations (and the commercial airline industry overall) were discursively, and historically, entwined with the physical bodies of the people doing this work (Ashcraft & Mumby 2004). Early women pilots were often talked about for the femininity and grace that they embodied, which helped foster a sense of flight as safe and pleasant. Concerned about threats to masculinity, however, the industry soon put forth the image of the pilot as masculine and in control by modeling his uniform on that of a ship's captain and reproducing contrasting traditional femininity by placing women in the cabin to attend to the comfort of passengers. Thus, we see how the "glass slipper" of occupations (Ashcraft 2013) that we discussed in the previous chapter is constructed through the combination of discourses and embodied labor.

Focusing more specifically on how individuals construct and navigate occupational identity (rather than how the occupation itself comes to claim an identity), other scholars have examined occupational identity for lawyers (Kuhn 2009), fundraisers (Meisenbach 2008), scientists (Wells 2013), entrepreneurs (Gill 2013; Gill & Larson 2014) and church planters (Ziemer 2016), highlighting how individuals construct identities in negotiation with others, as well as in negotiation with entrenched assumptions of what it means to do or identify with a particular occupation. Unsurprisingly, then, occupational identity has significant links to the scholarship on intersectionality (discussed in Chapter 4) and occupational prestige (noted in Chapter 6).

Variations on the Study of Identity Work

Overall, identity work is a broad term for describing a variety of research on identity that examines how individuals construct their identities. While often considering issues of power in the ways in which discourses are shaped or the ways in which they appeal, identity work research tends to privilege the individual as an active participant in shaping her/his identity. In the following sub-sections we explore some of the variations in the identity work research including: narratives, ideals selves, tensions and crisis.

Narrating identities. One variation of identity work research conceptualizes identities as ongoing narratives of the self. Theories that focus on individual agency often conceptualize identity as "something that has to be routinely created and sustained in the reflexive activities of the individual" (Giddens 1991, p. 52). As individuals navigate the many possibilities for defining the self, they do so by actively reflecting on their identities as projected, consider feedback from others either confirming or disconfirming their identities and then make choices. Individuals reflexively monitor their identities and bring forth certain identities in certain contexts as well as modify their identity narratives in the context of feedback.

A number of scholars drawing from the above assumptions focus on the narratives that individuals construct to answer the question Who am I? From this perspective, identities are the stories that people tell about themselves to themselves and to others. Such a view sees "identity construction as a continuous process of narration where both the narrator and the audience formulate, edit, applaud, and refuse various elements of the ever-produced narrative" (Czarniawska-Joerges 1994). In other words, we tell stories about ourselves that help to explain who we are in particular contexts and in particular roles. These stories, though, are not accepted by others (or even ourselves) without comparison to the stories of others or to other possible stories about ourselves. For example, Greg might say that he is the best skier in the world, but that story doesn't necessarily stick unless it matches with other narratives that support that story. (And unfortunately for him, that story definitely isn't supported.) Narrative identity work must be thought of as drawing from and negotiating with a wide range of possible identity narratives.

Some examples from the identity research demonstrate the narrating identities perspective. First, Ibarra and Barbulescu (2010) pulled from a wide range of identity research to suggest a narrative process for understanding identity work during role transitions at work. In their model, individuals who were faced with a role transition at work put forth various identity narratives or stories that attempt to explain this shift in identity in a way that also met their identity goals. They state:

> In successful transitions a coherent and compelling narrative set emerges from repeated interaction and revision, helping the narrator to internalize the new role identity and gain passage through the inclusion boundaries of the new work or occupational group. Alternatively, passages that do not find plausible or consistent narratives remain incomplete or fail. (p. 148)

Workers test possible identity stories in social situations and select the ones that gain the most traction – that seem the most "authentic" to others and subsequently to the self. The authors stress the process of testing and selecting identity narratives in social situations as key to understanding identity work.

A second example of the narrating identities perspective comes from Down and Reveley (2009) in their longitudinal study of a supervisor in an Australian industrial plant. Down and Reveley demonstrate how simply telling narratives of the self is not enough to form an identity. Combining narrative and interactionist theories (i.e., Goffman's dramaturgical perspective) of understanding the process of identity work, the authors suggest that narratives of the self are upheld, revised and rejected during the performance of such identities in particular contexts. For the manager they studied, acting like a manager and having his team members treat him like a manager during face-to-face interactions provided validity to the identity narrative that he was indeed a manager. In linking identity narratives with the performance of those identities, the authors suggest that "Most management identity researchers forget or ignore one of the most fundamental micro-sociological axioms: that confirming one's identity by displaying oneself in front of others is central to identity formation" (p. 398).

An emphasis on narratives or story telling underlies much of the research on identity work, whether the authors explicitly frame their work as a narrative approach or not (Alvesson 2010). From a discursive identity perspective, Discourses are the building blocks of identity and thus identity narratives (as discursive resources) play a major role in understanding how identities are formed and managed. In the following sections, although we discuss other ways to approach the study of identity work, narratives often remain an important component of conceptualizing identity work processes.

Ideal Selves/Possible Selves/Preferred Selves/Provisional Selves. Another variation of the identity work approach to understanding the formation and management of identities focuses on the idealizations and/or projections people make about their identities. Some scholars have focused on "possible selves" or future projections as to whom one might become, both positive, as in a successful future self, and negative, as in a lonely future self (Fiol 2002; Markus & Nurius 1986). Possible selves provide discursive resources that shape the options for identity work. Other scholars focus on "preferred selves" (Tracy & Trethewey 2005) or the

70

selves we prefer to be rather than the selves we may be forced to perform in some contexts. Other scholars use the term "ideal selves" (Giddens 1991; Wieland 2010) to focus on socially constructed ideals that help us determine which possible selves are the most appealing. Giddens (1991) defines the ideal self as the "self I want to be." The self we want to be is inherently linked to social identities and social preferences, as certain selves are more socially desirable than others. Finally, we also see "provisional selves" or experimental selves that are put forth by participants undergoing role transitions as a way of testing possible professional identities (Ibarra 1999). In each of these related framings, identity work is shaped by culturally sanctioned discourses that influence which identities are socially acceptable and desirable and which identities are less acceptable and less desirable. The identity work occurs as individuals reflexively engage these discourses in the context of trying to negotiate their identities for themselves and for others.

Looking more closely at ideal selves, Wieland (2010) frames ideal selves as "discursive resources that shape identity work and identity regulation" (p. 512). According to this approach, the discursive resources drawn upon for identity work are shaped socially as certain discourses are more appealing, or idealized, than others. In framing ideal selves as discursive resources, Wieland attempts to find a balance between the individual agency of actors in identity work and the regulation of identity by outside forces/discourses. That is, at the same time that ideal selves provide stories for identity work, they are also regulatory in the sense that they are cultural constructions that provide a limited scope of what is preferable. In making this move, Wieland purposefully bridges notions of personal identity and social identity by suggesting that socially sanctioned ideals become accepted as a way to construct personal identity. For example, in studying a local branch of a multinational research and development firm in Sweden, Wieland found two competing socially sanctioned narratives for defining a good worker. The first ideal worker discourse centered on "delivery" which meant the workers produced work in an opportune manner – got things done. The second ideal worker discourse focused on "well-being," as in having good quality of life both at home and at work. Organization members had to negotiate these two competing ideal selves in the context of their daily work lives (identity work) but in doing so were pressured to conform to both cultural ideals (identity regulation).

Identity tensions. Another way of understanding identity work processes comes from scholars who take a tension-centered approach (Trethewey & Ashcraft 2004). From this view, tensions are the norm in organizations, and so scholars should not be surprised to find they exist. For studies of identity in contemporary organizational contexts, it is thus unsurprising that organization members encounter tensions when trying to perform identity work. A key focus from this perspective is not how these tensions are resolved, as that is usually not possible, but rather how they are managed. As applied to identity work, this perspective points to the ongoing management of tensions as a primary process. Managing tensions between different identities or between different discursive resources for identity management becomes a key part of identity work.

Tension-focused scholarship focuses on how individuals manage the tensions they experience when trying to define themselves. For example, Pepper and Larson (2006) found that "cultural identity tensions" explained why members of a start-up company actively disidentified with an acquiring organization because its values were very different from the ones they had internalized at the start-up company. The acquiring company placed consensus-style decision-making as a core value of its culture, which aggravated members of the start-up company who preferred the quick, decisive decision-making of a strong formal leader. More than simple differences of opinion, these were core values that shaped the organizational identities of the participants and these differences prohibited the merger from working successfully. Other scholars have examined identity tensions in a variety of ways including occupational identity tensions among university fundraisers (Meisenbach 2008), identification tensions during organizational turmoil (Williams & Connaughton 2012) and "identity elasticity" in tensions as identities are socially constructed (Kreiner et al. 2015).

72

Forming and Managing Identities

Crisis, instability and change. Another theme in the identity work research focuses on how crisis, instability and change serve as the impetus for identity work (Alvesson et al. 2008). In some of the research, identity work is conceptualized as an ongoing process that occurs more or less continually during everyday interactions. For others though, identity work is triggered by events that call one's identity into question. For example, think about how graduating from university is a major life change that forces active identity work. An identity as a student and as linked to a university and all of the various clubs and organizations is often replaced by uncertainty. Lair and Wieland (2012) demonstrate that college students reconcile such uncertainty, specifically regarding questions about their major, with larger social narratives about getting a "real job." After graduation, some students start new jobs, some move to new cities and roughly 45% move back with their parents (Weissmann 2013). In each of these cases, a major life change forces former college students to rethink the question Who am I? They must distance themselves from parts of their old identity narratives, try out other possibilities and, ultimately, re-narrate parts of the self. In the research literature, there are numerous examples of crisis or change influencing identity work including Medved and Kirby's (2005) study of the identity crisis created when mothers first leave professional work to engage in full time child care, and Lutgen-Sandvik's (2008) exploration of "intensive remedial identity work" caused by instances of workplace bullying.

Overall, there exists a large amount of research that examines the formation and management of identity from an identity work perspective. The variations discussed in the previous pages show some of the ways in which scholars have tried to understand the processes associated with identity work and although no one approach is likely to emerge as dominant, each provides a useful way of conceptualizing parts of the process. Remember that all these identity work approaches tend to tilt toward the agency of the individual as an active participant in constructing her/his own identity and tend to highlight the discursive nature of the identity creation and formation process. Chapter 4 engages concepts related to identity work in more detail as we explore "fragmenting and intersecting" identities.

Identity Regulation

The third and final broad category from the organization studies research that attempts to explain the formation and management of identities is *identity regulation* (Alvesson et al. 2008; Alvesson & Willmott 2002). To place this approach within the framework discussed at the beginning of this chapter, scholarship that focuses on identity regulation or control tilts toward the influence of contextual factors such as "discourse, structure, powerful agents, [and a] messy world" (Alvesson 2010, p. 209) in shaping individual identities. While identity work focuses on the individual's ability to draw upon discourses to form a unique identity, identity regulation instead focuses on the ways in which our identities are created, shaped and influenced by powerful, outside forces. Individual agency, to the extent it is considered, manifests as constrained and limited from an identity regulation perspective.

Consider the process of finding your first "professional job" outside of college. In Western culture, there exists a popular Discourse that ascribes what a professional should look like and how a professional should act (Clair 1996). Your ability to find a professional job and to succeed in that job will be based, at least in part, on your ability to adopt a professional image (Cheney & Ashcraft 2007). From an identity regulation perspective, adopting this professional identity really isn't a choice that you get to make freely. Instead, most of us learn at an early age what it means to be a professional and, subsequently, what it means to be unprofessional. Schools and universities also instill students with a sense of what it means to be professional. In addition, we see representations of professional bodies, actions and discourses in the media. All of this adds up to a powerful sense of what it means (a Discourse) to be professional. If you want to get the job and succeed, then you usually have to adopt the identity of the professional. In this way our identities are largely controlled by widely accepted social Discourses that define what is appropriate/inappropriate or valid/invalid in a particular social setting.

From an identity regulation perspective, power is an important aspect of the process of identity formation and management. Influential organizations and groups have a large sway in shaping identities. At times this is purposeful and direct, as when organizations utilize corporate culture or self-directed teams (Barker 1999) in order to shape the identities and values and, thus, the actions of individuals. At other times this process occurs in a less direct manner, as when "Discourses of enterprise" (Alvesson & Karreman 2000) widely influence how workers construct their identities. From the identity regulation perspective, our identities are produced and controlled by powerful cultural discourses in society that serve to discipline the individual through identity. We will say much more about identity regulation in Chapter 5, as that is the focus of that entire chapter. At this point though, it is sufficient to see identity regulation as an alternative to the identity work perspective in that powerful forces/Discourses play a large role in forming our identities rather than individual agency.

Concluding Thoughts

This chapter explored how identities are formed and managed from three different perspectives: identification, identity work and identity regulation. Each of these approaches adds to our understanding of organizations and identity by focusing on different explanations for how identities are formed. The identification approach focuses on association and highlights the social aspects of individual identity. The identity work perspective focuses on the agency of individuals to construct their own identities and thus emphasizes the reflexive and communicative "work" that individuals engage in to narrate a sense of self. And finally, the identity regulation perspective suggests that powerful Discourses (endorsed by organizations) shape the identities of individuals and thus the control of identity formation is less about individual agency and more about how control is exercised through the shaping of identity. Although most scholars take some sort of middle ground position and note that agency and control are in tension in identity formation, understanding the distinctions between these perspectives is useful for understanding and classifying the literature on organizations and identity.

Discussion Questions

1. Where do you position your own beliefs about identity on the tension of insecurity versus coherence? Do you tend to see your own identity as more stable and enduring or more fragmented and becoming?
2. Where do you position your own beliefs about identity on the tension of agency versus regulation? Do you tend to see yourself as an agent capable of producing any identity you want or as something that is heavily influenced by powerful societal forces?
3. The term "work" suggests effort, so the phrase "identity work" indicates that forming an identity is something that requires effort and attention. In what ways do you engage in identity work, or do you see others engaged in identity work? What communicative interaction represents easily identifiable identity work? What communicative interaction represents more subtle identity work?
4. Think of previous experiences that you have had with work or volunteering. What were your feelings about the work or the organization? Would you say you identified with the organization? Why or why not? Were there aspects of the work with which you identified? Are there other organizations with which you identify – perhaps your University, church or a sports team? Why do you identify with these organizations, and how do you tend to perform this identification?
5. Reflect on an occupation to which you aspire or an organization where you would like to work. As far as you can tell, is there an "ideal self" attached to this occupation or organization? In other words, who do you think you'll be expected to be? Where did you learn about the ideal that is attached to the occupation or organization? Have you started to engage in identity work to this end?

4

Fragmenting and Intersecting Identities

Alek has always wanted to live in a place like Silicon Valley and work for a startup tech company like Uber or DraftKings. Taking his coding skills with him, Alek moves from his home country of Sweden to Silicon Valley and finds an entry-level programming position with a hot new startup. Alek is excited and he begins to settle in quickly. After some time, however, he realizes that being a programmer for a Silicon Valley start-up is not all that he was hoping for. He is good at his job and enjoys developing his talent, but he is put off by the extreme work ethic in "The Valley," where people seem to take it for granted that employees will work late hours and make work the focal point of their lives. Alek loves programming but wants to be in a situation that has expectations for work-life balance that will allow him to fulfill his other passions like long-weekend camping trips. Instead, Alek has become invested in showing his boss how dedicated he is, making sure his boss sees him working late and arriving early, so that he can make sure to get promoted and continue to do well. This has changed the experience of programming for Alek; in fact, being a programmer is a different kind of job in Silicon Valley than it was in Sweden, and this is making him rethink his choice to be a programmer. Alek is struggling with the different identities and expectations that are attached to being a programmer, working in the US versus Sweden and working in an extreme high-tech locale.

Alek's case is not unusual. In many places today, it is becoming *de rigeur* to study or work internationally, sometimes temporarily and sometimes permanently. Have you thought about whether you want to work outside of your region or country, and how do you think that would influence how you see yourself in regard to your occupation? Another scenario is to consider that you are a medical professional who is working in a new country. Zikic and Richardson (2015) did this, and explored how different norms regarding medicine, professionalism or work changed not only how medical professionals felt about their work but also their ability to identify with their work. Thus, although having international experience is considered a boon to a student's or employee's chances of being accepted to a desirable university or program, or to landing a great job, we can begin to see how it is possible that doing the same job in a different country is not the same at all. We will consider this and other issues of fragmented and intersecting identity in this chapter.

Identity in a Socio-Historical Context

Although it is safe to say that people throughout history have had to grapple with forming and managing their identities, we want to spend some time considering more recent and fundamental changes in contemporary society that necessitate changes in how we think about and "do" identity in the (late) modern world. Scholars have argued that we now live in a world in which there are numerous possible identities that compete to shape our sense of self, and any number of options for self-definition. There exists a complex array of factors that create the conditions for and shape identity, and we explore some of the most significant influences in creating the modern identity crisis.

Before we begin, we want to clarify why we believe it is important to understand identity scholarship within a socio-historical context. As we have discussed in previous chapters, identity is not merely one's own thoughts, personality or set of combined experiences. Rather, identity is influenced by the norms and conditions, as well as interpersonal interactions, ongoing in a particular time or place. Thus, we could observe that the possibilities for identity around, say, being an "entrepreneur" have changed over the past 50 years. To be called an entrepreneur in the middle of the twentieth century meant that one's motives and trustworthiness were being called into question; the entrepreneur at this time represented more of a "con-man"-type character. Since the 1970s and the birth of the personal computer, however, technology, capitalism and social norms have given new meaning to the term, so that identifying as an entrepreneur not only means something different now, but is an occupational label that often has a positive connotation and, in some places, is highly desirable.

We can also see, however, that even within the same time period (a synchronic rather than diachronic perspective), identity possibilities are different. A great example of this is in the earlier example of medical professionals. As Zikic and Richardson (2015) discuss, medical practitioners who change country context often grapple with different institutional discourses that shape their profession. In their research, medical professionals who migrated to the United States found that the differing professional norms and discourses of medicine meant that they struggled to find their identity as medical professionals, eventually ending up in a state of identity crisis. This example demonstrates how identity is not only historically, but is also socially and contextually, in flux. In this chapter, we address some of the larger, macro conditions of society that lead us to understand identity as fluctuating and fragmented, and some of the discursive and communicative approaches to understanding this.

Globalization

One of the major factors contributing to a less stable sense of the self in contemporary times is globalization. Processes of globalization, while underway for quite some time historically, have accelerated in the last half century with technological inventions such as commercial air travel, television, computers and the Internet. Because of these technologies, people are connected economically, socially, politically and organizationally in more ways than ever before with others around the globe. People around the globe share ideas, products, experiences, identities and even diseases at increasingly faster speeds. As we are writing this chapter, news arrives daily through the Internet to our homes in Missoula, Montana, United States and Auckland, New Zealand, about refugees fleeing oppressive regimes in Syria and Afghanistan to places like Greece, the UK, Germany and Scandinavia, with mixed results. The *Guardian* newspaper reported today that in just the first two months of 2016 alone, 100,000 refugees have sought entry to countries that are themselves struggling to manage the influx of such sheer numbers of people (Borger 2016). Such a mass migration is in addition to global occupational flows that see workers migrating to countries where their chances of employment, or opportunities to support their families, are greater.

That is, globalization, intensified by communication and transportation technologies, changes our notions of time and space. For most of human history, time and space were connected by the time it took to travel to a particular place, on foot or even on horse. The distance between the two largest cities in the United States, New York and Los Angeles is roughly 2,700 miles, and without technologies like trains, cars, planes, telephones and the Internet, that distance would take months, if not years, to travel. Today, co-workers interact instantaneously every day from New York to LA using internet video conferencing, and one can fly that distance in roughly five and half hours. While this is certainly not news to our readers, the interesting thing is what this does to our sense of the relationship between time and space. When time becomes disconnected from the boundaries of place, our sense of who we are in relationship to the rest of the world changes significantly. We are less likely to define ourselves according to the possibilities, positions and identity narratives of a particular place, but rather to seek out alternative narratives of identity from other places. For instance, a high school student in Mumbai, India can readily assess possibilities for occupational identity construction from places around India such as the high-tech sector in Bangalore or the movie industry in Bollywood, but also from around the world such as the high-tech sector in Silicon Valley or the movie industry in Hollywood. In fact, these regions in India and the United

States are already mutually influential as the values, practices and identities of various occupations are mimicked around the world. The compression of time and space decreases the chances that identities will be defined primarily by a particular place of birth, and increases the chances that people will create identities that draw from a wide array of possible identity narratives. This distanciation of time and space led sociologist Anthony Giddens to conclude that "for the first time in human history 'self' and 'society' are interrelated in a global milieu" (Giddens 1991, p. 32).

Mobility

A related key factor shaping the relationship between identity and organizations in contemporary society is increased mobility. The ability of people to relocate to places around the globe for different job or lifestyle opportunities (sometimes by choice, sometimes not) impacts identities. This is related to the previous section on globalization in that mobility is linked to increasing global competition for talent, advancing technologies that allow for more flexibility in work location and growing interconnectedness around the globe including climate refugees forced to migrate by global climate change. Increased mobility also means that some workers, particularly those in the "creative class," can voluntarily congregate in places that not only provide job opportunities, but also opportunities for social identity with people who share similar values. For example, if high-tech work can theoretically be done from anywhere, why do high-tech workers congregate in places like San Francisco's Bay Area; Austin, Texas; Boulder, Colorado; or the research triangle in North Carolina? Management scholar Richard Florida's research shows that creative class workers cluster in a relatively few number of regions globally and do so because they need to be around similarly creative people in order to achieve their full economic potential (Florida 2008). In addition, Florida finds that creative class workers congregate in places with high levels of openness – "defined by a communal sense of tolerance and acceptance of diversity" (p. 176). In other words, people choose to live in places that allow them to "be themselves" by enacting particular identities that align with that place, or locale. In Greg's research on why high-tech entrepreneurs moved to Missoula, Montana, he found that an outdoor recreation identity was a big part of why people choose to start businesses in Missoula (Larson & Pearson 2012). That is, these entrepreneurs chose to move to (or stay in) places that allowed them to enact an identity and where there were other people with similar identities. For identity and organizations, mobility matters as people with the available resources choose to congregate in places to fulfill identity needs. Note the underlying consideration of class and privilege here, though – a consequence is that it is increasingly the case that people without particular educational, intellectual and/or monetary resources cannot move into, or are forced out of, certain cities, thus leading to greater income stratification. The Atlantic Monthly observed that this has become the case, for instance, in Silicon Valley (White 2016).

Mobility also shows us how the lines between work and home are becoming more blurred. We can observe that in many cases, work and home have become enmeshed (Hochschild 1997), but a useful heuristic to see what this can look like is that of a "global care chain." A global care chain refers to the series of linkages that come together within industries and practices of care. As scholars like Arlie Russell Hochschild (Ehrenreich & Hochschild 2003) and Rhacel Salazer Parrenas (2001) have observed, care has become a commodification that is bought and serviced, leading to economies of care that span international borders. A clear example of a global care chain is in the story of Josephine, which is shared in Ehrenreich and Hochschild's book *Global Woman*. Josephine is a woman who originated from the Philippines and leaves her family to travel to the United States in order to become a nanny for an upper-middle class white family. To do this, however, Josephine leaves her own children in the care of a Philippino nanny, who has, in her turn, left her own children in the care of their eldest sister. This chain has three links around care: Josephine cares for the US children; the Philippino nanny cares for Josephine's children; and the Philippino's eldest daughter cares for her siblings.

Care chains such as this demonstrate how "work" identity and "home" identity are often blurred, and how even work that is largely invisible or not considered professional can nonetheless represent a pretty complicated work experience! People studying care chains often focus on the fragmentation of identity experienced by the migrating worker in the chain (Josephine, in the case above). In addition to adjusting to work that focuses on caring for another's children and missing one's own children, these workers grapple with the cultural and material issues that come with migration, which includes "basics" like learning a new language or even a new currency, and fitting in to a new community. Even beyond this, however, care chains are laden with additional complex implications for identity. Because the direction of labor in care chains typically moves from developing to developed countries, where wages are higher and migrants can therefore send more money home, scholars argue that a complicated hierarchy of gender, class and ethnicity is embedded into care chains, which impacts identity construction. That is, what we often see in such care chains are employees who are lower-income women of color working for employers who are higher-income white women, where both parties are navigating sensitive issues of care, family and work. Women working in care chains typically have one foot in their home country, where they try to keep up with the lives of their kids or extended family, and another foot in their new country, where their identity is in flux around the combined navigation of work, family, national culture and social identity.

Changes in the Nature of Work

A globalized world is characterized by rapid change, seen in the very nature of work and employment. There is a long history of academic scholarship on work in the modern world, beginning with Karl Marx's critique of work under industrial capitalism. From Marx's perspective, industrialization shifted work away from small, localized craft shops to large, mechanized corporations. The highly skilled craftsman, who apprenticed for years to learn the skills of a particular trade, was replaced by the assembly line worker, who performed low-skilled work for an hourly wage.

In this shift, work became less meaningful and less associated with a particular identity, leading to an overall weakening of a secure sense of identity.

Other changes in the nature of work also contributed to increased identity insecurity. The large bureaucratic corporations that arose in the United States and Europe after WWII, while portrayed as soulless in works like William H. Whyte's *Organization Man* and Arthur Miller's *Death of a Salesman*, at least provided a sense of occupational stability. For many workers, the job security and longevity that came with working for these organizations fostered identification with that organization. Today, the promise of long-term employment with one company is much more unlikely. Words like "business re-engineering" in the 1990s and "workforce re-balancing" or "rightsizing" today – all euphemisms for laying people off – characterize the tenuous corporate commitment to the workforce. Faced with an environment in which long-term employment is questionable, employees learn to look out for themselves, to shift jobs and loyalties as needed and to maintain vigilance for the next round of layoffs. In doing so, the potential for security and identity provided by stable employment is eroded.

In addition to the changes in the long-term commitment of employers and employees, recent technological advances are further impacting job descriptions, job security and the link between work and identity. Machines have long replaced lower-skilled workers, the very thing that Marx worried about. Today, though, even highly skilled workers are at risk of having their work altered or their jobs replaced by machines. For instance, IBM's supercomputer called "Watson," which initially received acclaim for defeating both chess masters and Jeopardy champions, is now being used to assist doctors in making key medical decisions. The Mayo Clinic is using Watson to pair cancer patients with clinical trials (Mastroianni 2014), the Cleveland Clinic is testing Watson's abilities to help doctors mine medical data to develop better diagnosis for patients (Townsend 2014) and IBM recently partnered with Apple Computer to allow Watson to analyze health data from its iWatch and iPhone health apps (Lohr 2015). Additionally, in higher education the technology of

Massive Open Online Classrooms, or MOOCs, offers the potential to deliver instructional content to huge numbers of students at little or no cost. Anyone with an Internet connection can now take courses from some of the best scholars at some of the most prestigious universities in the world, like Stanford or Harvard, for free. MOOC technology, though not putting colleges and universities out of business as some initially predicted (e.g. Selingo 2014), have influenced the ways in which classes are organized, taught and graded – potentially altering the nature of the work of professors and shifting the purpose of a university overall. For workers, as the nature of work changes, identity constructs related to that work are also potentially disrupted. An identity as a craftsperson, mechanic, doctor or house cleaner is often more tenuous in a world of rapid changes, layoffs and technological advancement. And overall, changes in the nature of work may lead to changes in the identities of workers (Ashcraft & Mumby 2004).

Blurring of the Work/Life Relationship

Advances in communication technologies and changes in the nature of work have led to a blurring of the relationship between work and personal life (Kirby, Golden, Medved, Jorgenson & Buzzanell 2003). Technologies like e-mail allow workers to work from anywhere, but in doing so this often pushes work into the realm of the home. For instance, as professors, we are almost as likely to be answering student e-mails from home in the evening as we are during the day on campus. This blurs the boundaries between home and work, which provides both benefits and pitfalls for workers and employers. In regard to identities, this blurring of work/life boundaries means that the separation between work identities and home identities may be less clear. For example, when a client calls on your mobile phone to discuss a recent proposal while you are at the same time driving your kids to soccer practice, considerable identity work must be done to strike a balance between both your work self with your parent self. In such cases the work self or the home self are not necessarily tied to distinct times and places, but may rather be frequently shifted depending on the nature of the situation. In addition, the gender and occupational norms of the early-to-mid-twentieth century that helped foster and maintain a divide between work and home are becoming increasingly challenged and old-fashioned, leading to more women in the public, paid workforce and more men taking responsibility for child care and stay-at-home parenting (though still to a lesser extent than women). As gendered parenting roles such as these are blurred, identities become less stable and more in need of frequent negotiation and balancing.

The work of communication scholars demonstrates the tenuous and often commercially influenced identities of workers as they balance ideals of work and home life. Eleff and Trethewey (2006) argue that parenting magazines shape their advice to parents around expectations of being enterprising. They give the example of all the ways that parents must plan a child's birthday party to meet particular aesthetic and consumer expectations. Parents are therefore engaged in a back-and-forth between their own preferences and social expectations. In a different context, Wieland (2010) shows how expectations of what it means to be a good worker are tied to what it means to be a good *person* overall. Wieland's study of a Swedish workplace shows how national discourses of Swedish identity are woven into workplace interactions so as to police one's relative goodness both in, and beyond, the workplace.

Discursive Approaches to Identity and Fragmentation/Insecurity/Instability

Discursive approaches to understanding identity and organizations tend to frame identities as multiple and contested, given the underlying assumptions of these approaches. In Chapter 2, we set forth five principles of a discursive approach to identity and organizations, and in those five principles we see the foundations of a non-essentialist understanding of identity. In review, the five principles are: communication as constitutive, identities as discursively constructed and mediated, discourse/Discourse as

86

interrelated, identity and organizations as mutually constituted and power as shaping organization and identity. The first two principles acknowledge the constitutive power of communication to construct social realities, including identities and, as communicative constructions, these are open to revision and reconstruction in various ways. In addition, when we conceive of discourse and Discourse as interrelated (the third principle), this highlights the inherent tension between stability (Discourse) and change (discourse). The fourth principle – identity and organizations as mutually constituted – also speaks to the ways in which both identities and organizations are communicatively and simultaneously constructed to further suggest identities are not wholly stable. The last principle, power as shaping identities and organizations, while neither inherently essentialist or non-essentialist, allows for power to be seen as shaping identities but also offers up possibilities for resistance. Overall, these principles are consistent with a view of identities that are contested and must therefore be managed by the individual or group. Although scholars taking discursive approaches tilt toward stability or change, there is broad acknowledgement in the literature that the self is under construction and that there are many different possibilities for defining the self.

Real-Self↔Fake-Self

If we conceive of the self as having many possible identities, then are some of these identities more authentic, or "natural," than others? Communication scholars Sarah Tracy and Angela Trethewey (2005) answer this question through the concept of a real-self↔fake-self dichotomy and offer a useful analysis of this tension. They argue that there are many references in popular culture, especially in self-help books, television talk shows and websites, to finding your true self. They cite numerous self-help gurus like Dr. Phil, who argue that all humans have a "root core" and are capable of becoming the "person you always wanted to be" (p. 173). Such evidence suggests that in Western culture, there seems to be a sense among many people that we indeed do have a true or real self and thus also, potentially fake selves. Tracy and Trethewey assert that the "real-self↔fake-self dichotomy is alive and well in the popular imagination and vocabulary" (2005, p. 173), but is this distinction useful? In other words, what do people gain and/or lose when they think of themselves as having true selves and fake selves?

For Tracy and Trethewey, the popular distinction between real and fake selves is problematic for several reasons, and they use scholarship on emotion management to illustrate their point. In the emotion management literature, starting with Hochschild's (1983) ground-breaking research on flight attendants, there has been a distinction between a public self and private self. The public self is the self that the organization expects at work – often an emotional performance of smiles and happiness toward customers. The private self, in contrast, is often framed as the real self, or the "true" emotions and feelings one brings to the work place – the person behind the company-mandated smiles. In many organizational contexts, like caring work (e.g., teachers and nurses) or professional work (e.g., engineers and lawyers) employees are encouraged to align their private and public selves into a "real" self in service of the organizational mission. Tracy and Trethewey (2005) argue that this real-self (private)↔fake-self (public) distinction leads to self-discipline and organizational control as well as organizational burnout and cognitive dissonance.

Yet, looked at from a poststructuralist perspective, *all* identities are socially created, and so *all* identities are as real or as fake as other identities. We enact particular identities in particular contexts and all of these identities are part of a whole self. By treating what is a symbolic distinction as a real one, the real-self↔ fake-self dichotomy creates the conditions under which organization members engage in self-discipline in order to bend their real selves to support the organization, experience cognitive dissonance when forced to perform inauthentic selves in the context of work or burn themselves out when trying to invest all of themselves in the service of others. Overall, the consequences of the reification of this dichotomy in popular culture creates negative consequences for workers (Tracy & Trethewey 2005). If you think back on our discussion in Chapter 3, you can see how this dichotomy is a social

88

construction that serves certain interests and not others – the fake self is more celebrated as it is mobilized in the performance of (public, paid) work, thereby benefitting organizational interests more than, perhaps, one's personal or family interests.

As a counter to the real-self↔fake-self dichotomy, Tracy and Trethewey (2005) propose the metaphor of the "crystal" as a way to talk about identity. A crystal forms a unique whole but has many different facets, making it appear different depending on how one looks at it. In a similar way, identities have many facets, none more real than the next, each one representing a different part of the self. In forwarding this metaphor, Tracy and Trethewey offer it as a prescription for a better way to talk about the different selves we enact in different contexts in a way that avoids the pitfalls of the real-self↔fake-self dichotomy. They argue that:

> As a crystallized self, for example, an executive may worry less about being a nurturer at work and at home feel less constrained by notions of running an efficient, Taylorized ship; as a crystallized self, a police officer might be more cognizant of the ways in which his work has hardened him, and he might make more careful choices about spending his leisure time in contrasting contexts. (p. 187)

Overall, from a discursive perspective that highlights the social construction of identities through language, the crystallized identity approach takes seriously the idea that the way that we talk about identity matters in how people construct their identities. This approach sees the management of multiple identities as many different facets of a (real) self that are presented in different contexts.

Intersectionality

Another lens through which communication scholars examine identity as fragmented is that of intersectionality. Originating in the legal field by the scholar Kimberlé Crenshaw (1991), the concept was conceived as a way to highlight structural discrimination in the law, particularly where policies and practices overlooked intra-group difference. Specifically, Crenshaw argued that issues facing black women were made invisible by laws that saw gender discrimination *or* race discrimination, but not both simultaneously. Women of color who sought legal protection had to argue that their cases were grounded in one or the other kinds of discrimination, thus denying the complex ways in which race and gender were entwined and making it more difficult for black women to access legal support and services.

Intersectionality has therefore come to represent a way of understanding identity, and particularly privilege and oppression, as multi-faceted, rejecting the notion that identity and identity politics are constructed along a "single-axis framework" of *only* gender, class, race/ethnicity and so forth (Ashcraft 2011; Nash, 2008). Beyond this, there has been robust debate about how to best theorize the ways that multiple identities are experienced and which social identities "matter" as a result. Scholars in communication and discourse studies often take a postmodern or poststructural approach to intersectionality, which means that they theorize that not only are identity "categories" socially constructed, but they are also fluid and changing (though they may be experienced as stable). As Rebecca experienced when she moved to New Zealand, for instance, the concept or category of American is defined and mobilized differently than in the United States. Because of this, the way that she relates to others around her difference (in New Zealand) and sameness (in the US) shifts depending on where she is and with whom she is interacting.

For many organizational scholars, intersectionality further represents the entwining of multiple identities against the backdrop of the workplace and within the processes and structures associated with work. Scholarship has often examined how certain images of the ideal worker have been woven into the very notions of professional work (i.e., white, youthful men as the abstract worker) and the identities of particular occupations (e.g., what it means to be a nurse or physician), where people who do not fit these images may experience them in different ways. Vanessa Gamble, for instance, recalls that during her time as a medical student, students of color were often "mistaken (even by medical professionals) for janitors, maids, and dietary workers" (2000, p. 165) and she reflects that, as a physician: "I would not just be a physician, but a black woman physician. I recall thinking that if I had been a white woman, the patient would have mistaken me for a nurse rather than a maid" (pp. 167–168). Gamble's experience demonstrates how her developing occupational identity (as a medical student) is simultaneously entwined with assumptions about the social categories she inhabits.

Gamble's experience illuminates further how intersectionality is something that is accomplished in interaction, or "done" through identity scripts in which we are positioned as similar and/ or different from others (West & Fenstermaker 1995). Regimes of inequality circulate and arrange occupations and organizations (Acker 2012), but it is in conversation and interaction that social and occupational stereotypes inform how "actors embody and negotiate a complex composite of salient social identities (gender, race, class, ability, age, and sexuality, as well as professional roles and disciplinary identities), which variously invoke degrees of privilege and oppression" (Ashcraft & Allen 2003, p. 25; Allen 2011; Parker 2014). This way of understanding intersectionality has been modeled by Adib and Guerrier (2003) in their study of how hotel workers negotiate ethnicity, gender and class. They showed how hotel workers negotiated both differences and similarities in their social identities, for instance, in the story of a woman who deflected sexual (i.e., gender-based) harassment from a male co-worker, by emphasizing their shared ethnicity.

An anti-categorical approach to intersectionality (McCall 2005), however, provides a more discerning foundation for a discourse perspective on intersectionality. This approach challenges the notion that there are established categories of difference that are always significant, or that the experience of certain categories will be experienced in the same ways (by one person or across people). Drawing attention to the need to challenge our reliance on categories of identity, James McDonald (2015) advocates a queer theory approach to intersectionality that examines the construction of identity(ies) against the backdrop of what has been constructed as normal. Because organizational and occupational discourses, as well as practices, are predicated on an enduring but socially constructed sense of what is logical and normal, anti-categorical intersectionality scholars may examine how a variety of identities may play out against and within the workplace.

So what, then, makes some part of our identity something that "matters" if our goal is to reject categories? Brenda Allen (2011) has answered this question by articulating that some differences "make a difference" and some do not, and what makes them make a difference or not is the context, including the people with whom you interact. Thus, some aspect of yourself might seem to matter in one context, but in another may be no big deal. If you identify as gay, lesbian, bi-sexual or transgendered, for instance, your sexual or gender identity (as it may be) may become a background part of who you are when you are with friends to whom you are out or in a workplace that actively supports a range of sexual identities. That is, what might make you different from others (as a sexual minority) in other facets of your life may be interpreted and experienced as a relation of sameness, and therefore this difference may not make a difference. Ultimately, what comprises your intersectional identity can be any number of things – what happens to make a difference or create relations of sameness in a given situation.

Recognizing this, organization scholars have begun to articulate intersectionality as the negotiation of credibility and legitimacy in relation to the way that social privilege and disadvantage have been woven into disciplines, institutions and fields; the identities of particular occupations; and workplaces themselves. In an early use of intersectionality, for instance, Angela Trethewey (2001) interrogated work at the intersection of age, ethnicity and class when she studied professional, middle-aged white women. She argued that women in professional work are encouraged to remain relevant by styling themselves in ways that present a particular image of success. Not only does this represent intersectional experiences for middle-aged (white) women, but it calls to the fore how class may also become part of one's assemblage of identities.

The enactment of intersectionality in the workplace has been explored around language and national identity, as well, and it is here that intersectionality as a demonstration of competence comes most to the fore. Celeste Wells (2013) has argued, for instance, that language is a form of human capital and one's ability to speak well (described as using correct grammar, adopting a mainstream accent and pace of speech and appropriately demonstrating eye contact and even silences) represents a performance that is accomplished and evaluated in the workplace. In her study of highly educated foreign-born chemists working in the United States, Wells (2013) found that it was not enough in their organizations that they spoke English but that their competence was judged based on their ability to speak *US-style* English, regardless of the fact that they were nonetheless highly skilled. We can see from Wells' study that, in the context of US research, one's ability to perform the language of US English represents economic, social and symbolic power. In a later study, Wells and colleagues (Wells, Gill & McDonald 2015) highlighted how language proficiency as a difference further interacted with education and tenure (or the length of time in a job) and national origin. This follow-up study suggested that intersectionality is comprised of a latticework of identities, representations and performances, where some are more or less prominent at different times and with different people.

Boogaard and Roggeband (2010) take this conversation further to show how the accomplishment (or negotiation) of intersectional competence can be infused with paradoxes. In their analysis, Boogaard and Roggeband observe that police offers may downplay the marginalized aspects of their identity (in the case of this study site, being a woman or ethnic minority) to establish the ways in which they possess privilege (e.g., by distinguishing themselves as an executive officer rather than an administrative officer), or they may highlight how their unique differences as minorities provide them with additional competencies that police officers in the majority do not possess (e.g., speaking much-needed different languages). Boogaard and Roggeband articulate the paradox as a case where: (a) highlighting one's competent identity also reproduces the marginalization of other dimensions of identity; and (b) those identity characteristics that are often deemed inappropriate are also mobilized in special or unique situations (e.g., needing to connect to someone as a woman officer or speak a language other

93

than the dominant one) that are then used to demonstrate highly valuable competence.

Concluding Thoughts

This chapter began by explaining the conditions of contemporary society that create identity fragmentation or the existence of multiple identities. The management of multiple identities thus constitutes a primary identity process and challenge of modern life. Organizations play a prominent role both in creating identity choices and in sanctioning certain identities as more prestigious or desirable. In addition, this chapter explored ways of thinking about identity fragmentation including the crystallized self and intersectionality, which attempt to explain the ways in which multiple identities intersect and combine in particular contexts to shape the experience of the self. We argued that it is increasingly important for scholars to consider the intersections of various identities, including those outside of the container of the organization, when studying identity and organizations. In the next chapter, we expand this discussion of multiple identities by exploring how identities are regulated and resisted.

Discussion Questions

1. What narratives in modern society make it more difficult for you to think of yourself as having a coherent, stable identity? What messages do you regularly hear that make you aware of different identity possibilities? What future possible selves are most appealing to you at this point in your life?
2. In what ways do you engage the "real-self↔fake-self" dichotomy in your own life? In other words, which selves do you consider more real? Why? Which selves do you consider less real? Why? How do societal expectations influence your beliefs about what is a real or true self? What are the negative consequences of trying to find a "real" self?

3. What are the identity intersections that define your own identity? Describe two or three social identities that you enact in framing and accomplishing your own identity. How/why are those intersections consequential? Consider your answer against the backdrop of your ideal or actual occupation, including, perhaps, your role in a global care chain. Do you seek to highlight or downplay particular elements of your identity in relation to your ideal or actual work?

4. Think about experiences you may have had when living, working or traveling in another region or country. What was easy and/or difficult about this experience? What assumptions did people make about you around social identity? Were these assumptions expected or unexpected, and why?

5. Look through any major newspaper today to find stories (and often very strong opinions!) about global flows of migration. Do stories tend to focus on immigrants (people entering a country) or emigrants (people exiting a country), and how are each described or pictured? Is the intersectionality of migrant identities an explicit or implicit part of the description, and if so, how? How often do these stories discuss the work, or occupations of, migrants, and in what ways?

5

Regulating and Resisting Identities

At one aerospace company called JAR in the Rocky Mountain West of the United States, managers faced a dilemma. The company's success in the past was largely attributed to their ability to solve the most difficult technical problems and produce the most reliable instruments, regardless of the cost or time, but government and commercial customers were now asking for something else. Customers demanded cost and schedule to be at least as important as the performance of the instruments. NASA even had a new mantra, which characterized this shift: "Faster, Better, Cheaper." For managers at JAR, this wasn't simply about changing priorities, it was about changing identities.

JAR managers and employees valued technical excellence as a key discursive resource in shaping their identities. They boasted of building instruments that long exceeded their expected life spans and prioritized engineering excellence. For employees and managers, technical excellence wasn't just a saying, it was rather part of who they were – part of their work identities. So when customer needs changed, it was not an easy adaptation for JAR members to change their value priorities. Changing their values to meet customer needs meant changing identities, identities that had provided JAR members with status, self-worth and a sense of purpose (Larson & Tompkins 2005).

The concept of identity regulation helps to explain these struggles of JAR members, and also sheds light on some puzzles of human motivation. For instance, why is it that we push ourselves to complete things in ways that no one actually asks us to? How is it that students will stay up late to study for an exam, but teachers could never require this of them? Or, why do people in self-directed work teams often work harder than if they were working for a traditional boss? This chapter shows identity regulation as a powerful form of social and organizational control. We begin with a discussion of the evolution of control systems in modern organizations that leads to a contemporary focus on identity. Next, we explore how identities are created or produced. Finally, we articulate resistance as a constant companion to control and detail how resistance counters efforts to control identities.

Control and Identity

In contemporary organizations, organization members are often controlled through their hearts and minds rather than through direct forms of discipline. The ancient Greek philosopher Heraclites argued, "Character is fate." What he means by this is that who you are determines what happens in your life. Many identity theorists make a similar assertion – that your identity, though constituted, influences how you act and what is made available to you. Identity has therefore become understood by many as the primary battleground for control in contemporary society and contemporary organizations.

Control is an inherently communicative process according to the "double interact" of control (Tompkins & Cheney 1985). In its simplest form, an interact can be thought of as a message and feedback to that message, and a double interact is when you have two message and feedback cycles. Control happens when a double interact is created from the following three components: (1) directions or instructions are given; (2) employee actions are monitored; and (3) rewards and punishments are dispersed. The first interact is that in which directions or instructions are given, thus constituting the message, and employee actions are monitored accordingly, thus providing feedback on how well the message was received. The second interact in the double interact is that in which monitoring employee actions is the message, and rewards or punishment represent the feedback. In the first interact, the organization provides a message and measures how well the employees respond, and in the second, the employees provide a message (through how well they perform), and receive feedback on their performance. This way of thinking about control – where one person or party successfully directs another person or party through messages and feedback – makes it clear how communication is a central dimension of control.

Types of Organizational Control

Undoubtedly, organization is not possible without some form of control. Barnard (1938) defined a formal organization as a "system of consciously coordinated activities or forces of two or more persons" (p. 73). Achieving coordination for the purpose of attaining a shared goal requires control. Thus, although control is often negatively characterized, we can see how, as a concept, it helps us to theorize how people (i.e., organizations, teams, groups) come together to harness their shared energies in order to achieve goals. Without control, we could argue, there is chaos – even in its most mild form, control provides structure, manifests agreement and guides action and decision-making. Given the significance of control to organizations and the process of organizing, it makes sense to begin with a brief history of control in modern organizations.

Richard Edwards (1979), in his book *Contested Terrain*, examined management practice since the industrial revolution and identified three primary forms of control. As the title of the book indicates, Edwards viewed the workplace as something that was inherently contested between workers and managers/owners. Put simply, he observed that it is likely in the best interests of workers to put in as little effort as possible and receive the most pay possible, while it is likely most beneficial to owners if employees work their hardest but get paid as little as possible. Although human motivations and relationships are more complex than this simple statement, it is hard to deny that there are some inherent conflicts in the employee/owner relationship. Given this contested terrain, Edwards argued that control was always paired with resistance. Control produces resistance, which leads to new forms of control. Edwards termed this the "dialectic of control," where dialectic refers to the way in which two opposing forces can be nonetheless linked to each other. He argued, therefore, that control and resistance must always be understood in relationship to each other, as they are fundamentally part of the same process. As we examine Edwards' three types of control and add another, we will see that resistance plays a part in each new form of control.

The first type of control that Edwards identified was simple control. Simple control is direct supervision of employees by managers. Think about a small business where the owner is present most of the time, giving instructions, monitoring what employees do and doling out rewards and punishments. This was the most common form of control in the early part of the industrial revolution, but it became increasingly difficult to enact as the size of organizations grew (imagine trying to directly supervise, say, fifty or more people!). As a result, owners hired managers, or "foremen" as they were termed, in order to carry out the wishes of the owner. The foremen acted in the interests of the owners to enact the message-feedback interact we discussed earlier, providing instructions, monitoring workers and dispensing rewards and punishments. Yet, as organizations continued to grow, this type of control became increasingly problematic from the perspective of the owners. First, it was hard for owners to control the foreman. Second, workers resisted the often-arbitrary control of the foremen. The securities we take for granted in modern bureaucracies, such as that employers need cause to fire employees, were non-existent in the simple control system of this era. Instead, foremen could simply hire those they liked and fire those they did not. The labor strife around the turn of the twentieth century, which included numerous examples of large worker strikes, like the US Steel Strike and the Pullman Rail Strike, formed in response to numerous and wide-spread dissatisfaction with simple control, including the way workers were treated by foremen. Yet, as simple control was resisted, owners came up with new ways to control workers.

The next form of control Edwards discussed is technical control. Technical control involves regulating workers by controlling the physical structure of work. The classic example of early technical control is Henry Ford's "endless conveyor belt" – the assembly line. The assembly line exemplifies technical control because the directions/instructions for work were largely determined by the technology. If an owner wanted production to increase, he could speed up the assembly line, which would necessitate that workers also speed up. From the owner's perspective, technical control had the added benefit of reducing social communication among workers. Instead of a person delivering a part to another person, workers often stood in one place, socially isolated, as the *machine* moved parts from person to person. By reducing social interaction, technical control not only created greater efficiencies but it also reduced some possibilities for collective resistance.

Despite the success of Ford's assembly line and the continued use of assembly lines today, workers effectively resisted technical control as a primary form of control. A small number of workers could "sit down" and refuse to do their part of the work, thereby forcing the entire assembly line to shut down. Sit down strikes, organized by unions, proved a successful way for workers to resist technical control. Another weakness of technical control centered on the limitations of technical systems to do more than provide directions and instructions. The monitoring of work and the dispensing of rewards and punishments still required managers or foremen, who themselves, as we noted, were difficult for owners to control.

Bureaucracy represents the third type of control to emerge in the modern workplace. Bureaucracy comprises a rational-legal system of rules that govern all three aspects of the control process. Direction and instructions, monitoring of performance and dispensing of rewards and punishments all fall under the jurisdiction of the bureaucratic system. Managers are still needed, but their behavior is significantly constrained by bureaucratic rules and procedures. For example, employees in a bureaucracy are governed by job descriptions and other policies that determine how employees are directed, evaluated and disciplined. Many of us are familiar with a common policy regarding coming to work late, which involves managers giving a verbal reprimand on the first instance, a written reprimand on the second instance, and a more severe reprimand (including firing) on the third instance. Thus, although managers are still needed in a bureaucratic system, their discretionary control over discipline is largely inhibited by the rational-legal bureaucratic system.

Although bureaucracy continues to influence contemporary organizations in significant ways, limitations and resistance to bureaucracy reduce its effectiveness as a system of control. Bureaucracies produce stability, but they do not necessarily increase performance or productivity. Competing in a globalized society often requires efforts from employees that go well beyond what is required in bureaucratic rules and procedures. Bureaucracies are also slow to adapt to changing conditions, as a top-down hier-archical system does not have the flexibility to respond to rapid changes. Workers on the front lines, who are often the closest to customers, often cannot make quick decisions in a bureaucratic system that would otherwise benefit the customers. In addition, workers can resist bureaucracy by only doing their jobs as required by their job descriptions – nothing more. Because of these limitations, alternative modes of control were developed that largely focus on controlling identities.

Thus, in addition to Edwards' (1979) three types of control, Tompkins and Cheney (1985) added another type of control: concertive control. Concertive control works through identification with the organization or its values, and peer enforcement of those values. Unlike a bureaucratic system, which operates through an external system of rules and policies, a concertive system operates by capturing the hearts and minds of employees. Specifically, concertive control relies on the building of a value consensus among organization members that organization members internalize as their own (Barker 1993; 1999). Through the process of identification, organization members either adopt the values of the organization that managers persuade them to follow (Tompkins & Cheney 1985) or develop their own value consensus (Barker 1999), often under the strategic direction of management (Sewell 1998). The term "concertive" suggests that the organization members act "in concert," or together, in that they share a system of values and hold each other accountable to those values. In concertive control, the three essential elements of a double interact control system are shaped by the shared value system of the group. That is, directions and instructions are largely determined by the values that the group holds, monitoring occurs as organization members monitor each other and hold each other to group standards, and rewards and punishments are doled out by the members themselves or by managers in conjunction with the core values of the group. The locus of control in a concertive system shifts away from the rules and procedures of the bureaucracy to the shared values of the members. Can you think of a student club or team with which you're involved that operates by creating shared expectations and rewards or punishments for each other like this? Perhaps in your club or team, strong identification essentially functions as a powerful mechanism of control.

The story of XEL Communications demonstrates the power of identification for controlling worker decision-making. In a study of workers at XEL, an electronics board manufacturing facility, Jim Barker (1993; 1999) showed how concertive control works. In an attempt to remain competitive in an age of increasing global competition, XEL management decided to implement self-directed work teams. One morning, workers showed up to a rearranged working environment where equipment was configured so that teams of workers could each complete all parts of the assembly process. Workers were divided into the red, the blue and the white team and instructed to manage themselves to produce electronics boards for their customers. In his research at XEL during this transition period, Barker found that the organization members began the process of establishing self-direction by making various "ought to" statements such as "we ought to take care of our best customers first" or "we ought to show up to work on time." These kinds of statements eventually became part of the value consensus of the group. In other words, these statements were internalized by members of the group, meaning that they accepted these values as their own, and these values therefore became part of the group's culture. As a result, members disciplined themselves and others according to the value consensus of the group. In one example, Barker tells of a woman named Sharon who comes to work late because of family issues and is confronted by the group. Sharon is collectively admonished by her peers and told how her tardiness affects the entire group. Despite that this situation sounds harsh, and is likely one that many of us want to avoid, it provides great insight into the power of concertive control as peers implement it.

Normative Forms of Control

In contemporary organizations, in many contexts, identity serves as a key battleground for organizational control. The previous section examined concertive control as one conceptualization of this type of control, but it is one of many related conceptualizations as to how identity regulation takes place. In their analysis of the history of management discourse, Stephen Barley and Gideon Kunda (1992) distinguished between rational and normative rhetorics of control that pattern throughout the history of management ideology. Rational rhetorics are those that appeal to the logic, coherence and reason of a larger system (of which workers are only one part), such as those that were driven by the application of scientific thinking to management practices in the early 1900s (e.g., "Taylorism"), and in which "employees were said either to understand the economic advantages of an efficient system or to be powerless to resist a well-designed structure" (p. 384). Normative rhetorics, on the other hand, refer to the messages and ideals that promote "cohesion and loyalty as the ultimate source of productivity," where, "as sentient, social beings, employees were said to perform more diligently when they were committed to a collective whose ideals they valued. Control therefore rested on shaping workers' identities, emotions, attitudes and beliefs" (p. 384). The term "normative control" thus serves as a general description of a number of similar conceptualizations as to how control is manifested through identity. The next part of this chapter explores normative control beginning with the kind of work where this type of control is prevalent.

In organization studies, beginning with the culture movement of the 1980s, scholars have increasingly explored identity regulation as a form of control in contemporary workplaces. While simple, technical and especially bureaucratic strategies of control remain influential in some work contexts and in some occupations, more normative forms of control exist in variations of work framed as "knowledge work" (Drucker 1994), "creative class" work (Florida 2002), teamwork (Barker 1999) and professional work (Kuhn 2009). These kinds of work are typically less hierarchical, more participative, more flexible and involve a combination of mental and physical capacities. Florida (2002) stated, "The key difference between the Creative Class and other classes lies in what they are primarily paid to do. Those in the Working Class and the Service Class are primarily paid to execute according to plan, while those in the Creative Class are primarily paid to create and have considerably more autonomy and flexibility than the other classes to do so" (p. 8). Creative class jobs include those in areas of "science and engineering, architecture and design, education, arts, music and entertainment" along with others in finance, business, law and healthcare (Florida 2002, p. 8). Although such jobs often allow for more freedom, flexibility and participation, control is nonetheless present in them, often manifesting in how identities are regulated. We thus turn to a discussion of identity regulation as an outgrowth of normative control.

Producing Identity Regulation

Identity regulation, broadly, "encompasses the more or less intentional effects of social practices upon processes of identity construction and reconstruction" (Alvesson & Willmott 2002, p. 625). In other words, identities are regulated when social beliefs or practices impact who we are, and this can include organizational beliefs or practices. Identities are regulated as the interests of organizations, institutions, professions and so forth, attempt to shape how members of these groups think of themselves and their work and workplace. Some interests have more influence than other interests, which means that *power* is a key factor in identity regulation. Although individuals may choose among a range of potential Discourses through which to define their identities, some of these Discourses are more appealing (or, more powerful) than others. Scholars who focus on identity regulation rather than identity work (which we discussed in the previous chapter) therefore tend to emphasize the ways in which identities are determined or produced by powerful interests. Although few in organization studies would argue today that identities are totally determined (Zoller 2014), there is still the tendency for research to tilt toward either more deterministic (meaning identities are determined by those in power) or agentic (meaning that we get to construct our own identities) interpretations of identity construction. Most often in scholarship on identity regulation, the tendency is to tilt toward determinism with attention to agency – in other words, acknowledging that people can make choices (to sometimes varying degrees) in identity construction, but stressing the powerful influence of Discourse that itself constrains such choice (Alvesson & Karreman 2000). There are a number of different explanations for the ways in which this occurs, and the next section explores some of the most significant conceptualizations.

Foucauldian Approaches

Drawing on the work of Foucault, much identity research seeks to unpack the ways in which Discourses produce identities. In his work, Foucault articulated the relationship between power, knowledge and subjectivity as one where, taken together, power and knowledge produce what we "know" as a society, and this knowledge makes available certain individual subject positions. In Foucault's articulation, those in power determine what counts as legitimate knowledge, leading to the (re)production of large scale and enduring Discourses, as well as subject positions – which can be likened to the roles we play in our everyday lives – made available and desirable by such Discourses. For example, in Western society the subject position of "professional" is created through Discourses that shape knowledge of the correct ways to act within the capitalist economic system. The very concept of "professional" suggests appropriate and inappropriate ways to communicate, act and think, as Jacques (1996) notes: "One might think of professionalism as a language, a system of objects, concepts and normative practices within which occupations and individuals must work if they are to successfully claim professional authority" (p. 90). Locating oneself within the Discourse of the professional provides affordances for identity, but also constrains potential actions and decisions.

Discourses that sanction (essentially give permission for – or not) certain types of behaviors and attitudes largely shape what we know as individual identity. Flipping the traditional understanding of identity as inherently individualistic on its head, a Foucauldian approach to identity suggests that Discourse precedes identity in that identities are produced as people locate themselves within various Discourses (Alvesson 2010). That is, rather than beginning with an individual who has the ability to create a unique identity, this perspective suggests that the Discourses are there first, and that they largely influence who we are. Imagine, for instance, how you might be different if you grew up under, or interacting with, different Discourses such as those attached to different cultures, religions and/or value systems. This perspective emphasizes the ways Discourse produces identities rather than the ways individuals carve out unique selves.

Another key concept from Foucault that adds to this perspective on identity regulation is that of discipline – not only in the sense of a punishment or reprimand, but also in the sense of how sets of ideas guide and regulate thinking and being (e.g., one's major in college brings with it different assumptions and ways of viewing the world, be it in communication studies, history, chemistry, gender studies or conservation management). Foucault contends that "Disciplines characterize, classify, specialize; they distribute along a scale, around a norm, hierarchize individuals in relation to one another and, if necessary, disqualify and invalidate" (1977, p. 223). Foucault sought to understand modern forms of punishment that attempted to "normalize" some kinds of attitudes and behavior and alienate others. For instance, the discipline of modern medicine normalizes what it means to be a healthy person (e.g., what constitutes a normal blood pressure, prescribed definitions/recommendations for obesity, mental illness as something abnormal), and in doing so shapes attitudes and behaviors regarding health. In other words, people discipline themselves to that which is prescribed by the labels, categories and Discourses of a particular discipline. Such labels and categories, such as that of "bipolar" in psychiatry, shape one's reflexive sense of subjectivity. According to Townley (1993):

> These labels may become incorporated into an individual's self-assessment, the means through which individuals identify their feelings and behavior to themselves and others. It is perhaps in this way that Foucault's (1977a: 170) statement that "disciplines 'make' individuals" makes most sense. (p. 535)

As an individual draws upon various Discourses to reflexively understand her sense of self, then, those Discourses are also doing the work of producing that identity.

Related to discipline is Foucault's concept of self-subordination. Here, individuals are theorized as participating in disciplining themselves, or self-managing, in the service of organizational ends. Deetz (1998) states:

> Through self-surveillance and control of their bodies, feelings, dress, and behaviour, [people] use themselves for their own strategized employment and careers movement (Foucault, 1977b ...).This self-management frequently benefited managerial interests more than company or employee ones. Self-management is management of the inner world along normative lines through the use of self and professional knowledge. (p. 164)

Self-subordination manifests in a wide variety of situations in which employees adopt certain Discourses and then hold themselves accountable to those Discourses. For example, in her research on a cruise ship, Tracy (2000) noted that employees would do "tricks" like cart-wheels to make an impression on passengers with the hopes of garnering positive comments on customer surveys. The ever-present "smile" that cruise ship employees always wear is another example of self-subordination. Tracy notes the dark side of such self-subordination where, for instance, a female employee feigned ignorance, rather than express anger, to fend off the inappropriate sexual advances of an older male passenger. In an organizational culture taught to satisfy the needs of customers and with an attitude of "we never say no," such habits of discipline can create obstacles to more agentic responses to such inappropriate behavior. Tracy (2000) also notes that such self-surveillance, such as the constant monitoring of emotions to project an energetic and positive self, can lead to employee burnout.

Approaches for explaining identity regulation that draw from Foucault thus emphasize the ways in which knowledge and power intersect in a given time and place to produce particular subjectivities (i.e., accepted roles, attitudes or behaviors). Normative control is created as individuals subordinate themselves according to their identities, which are themselves produced by Discourses. Many different discursive approaches to understanding identity regulation draw from these ideas to understand how normative control happens.

Broad Discourses

As the previous section detailed, Foucauldian approaches provide insight into how Discourses function to regulate identities. In this section, we explore an example of a key big "D" Discourse in society that shapes, organizes and disciplines identities. There are many big-D Discourses we could discuss here, and the goal of our exploring one in detail is to illuminate how broadly accepted ideologies, worldviews and cultural norms (i.e., Discourses) shape who we are in the context of both work and life.

Neoliberalism and the Discourse of enterprise. An instructive example for how broad discourses shape and regulate identities is found in neoliberalism. Catalyzing in the 1970s, neoliberalism has become a dominant ideology throughout the world (Harvey

2005). At its core, neoliberalism stresses the superiority of the free market for regulating economic and social systems. According to this theory, "human well-being can best be advanced by liberating individual entrepreneurial freedoms and skills within an institutional framework characterized by strong private property rights, free markets and free trade" (Harvey 2005, p. 2). In neoliberalism, governments are needed to maintain currencies, enforce laws and ensure open markets, but overall, government intervention is viewed as negative. As a result, the rise of neoliberal ideology has seen a corresponding decrease in government regulation of economic, political and social life. For instance, banking deregulation, carried out during the 1980s and 1990s, greatly reduced the limitations placed on financial industry. Overall, the widespread ascendance of neoliberalism as a dominant discourse is most evident in that these ideas have become a common frame for interpreting the world for many people – consider, for instance, the observation that the telos of university education, broadly, has shifted from teaching students to be citizens to teaching students to be entrepreneurs (Godwyn 2009). Neoliberal values greatly influence not only the (de)regulation of the capitalist economic system, but all human relationships. Recent – and frequent – calls for schools, hospitals and governments to be more attuned to the needs of their customers demonstrates the widespread influence of this Discourse.

A subset of neoliberalism that provides insight into how such Discourses are taken up for identity regulation focuses on the "Discourse of enterprise." Organizational scholars have explored the Discourse of enterprise and noted its expanding influence. The Discourse of enterprise references a cluster of ideas centered around the ideal of the "sovereign consumer" (du Gay & Salaman 1992) as the center of modern life. The consumer replaces the citizen in contemporary society as the fundamental interpretive lens for understanding individual and collective action. Under this lens (or Discourse), everyone is largely remade as a consumer, including students, patients, employees and citizens – and even viewers of reality TV (Woodstock 2014), CrossFit gym-goers (James & Gill 2015) and parents (Eleff & Trethewey 2006). Even in what would otherwise seem to be traditional organizations, employees are branded as consultants who answer to customers, who are themselves often other employees in the organization. As a result of a commitment to the "customer," these rebranded consultants work harder and discipline themselves in severe ways in response to customer needs (Deetz 1998). Overall, this discourse privileges "enterprising qualities – such as self-reliance, personal responsibility, boldness and a willingness to take risks in pursuit of goals" (du Gay & Salaman 1992, p. 628).

In the Discourse of enterprise, the self is largely seen as an entrepreneurial project with the individual responsible for making her or himself into an object of continual growth through self-discipline. The "enterpreneur of the self" Discourse suggests that successful and productive individuals remain continuously involved in improving their own human capital, through such things as increased education or gaining new skills (du Gay & Salaman 1992). Just as success in a commercial enterprise relies on constant improvement, the entrepreneur of the self also strives for internal growth to make themselves more valuable and marketable to employers. The proliferation and popularity of self-help books is evidence of this focus on self-improvement (Holmer Nadesan & Trethewey 2000). Overall, the Discourse of enterprise functions to shape identity as it serves as a widespread Discourse that helps to define what is normal, natural and, thus, deemed successful, in our society. For understanding identity regulation, the Discourse of enterprise serves as an exemplar for how certain Discourses can function to regulate identity at the individual level.

Locale-Specific Discourses

Although broad Discourses are influential in shaping and regulating identities, other, more locale-specific discourses (Kuhn 2006) may also regulate identities. Locale-specific discourses refer to common ways of understanding or knowing that are developed in particular geographic, temporal and social contexts. These are smaller, localized versions of big "D" discourses which emerge from the values, norms, rituals, practices and affordances of a particular culture and place. These locale-specific discourses influence the regulation of identity in local contexts. Tim Kuhn (2006), for instance, showed how two different organizations developed very different understandings of the proper use of time, based on the influence of different locale-specific discourses. In an organization referred to as DPC, members developed an "intense" work ethic from professional Discourses that valued dedication to work and local discourses that promoted public and environmental accountability. In an organization referred to as MLF, a "lifestyle" approach to work time commitments was derived from professional Discourses that encouraged workers to choose overwork as a *temporary* necessity and locale-specific discourses that supported a balanced work-life relationship. Worker identities were therefore not only influenced by organizational and professional influences, but the locale-specific discourses of public and environmental accountability (in the case of DPC) and work-life balance (in the case of MLF) also influenced the construction of "locally approved" work identities. As Kuhn argues, both cases highlight how identities at work are derived from an "array of discursive possibilities . . . constrained by both organizations and locales" (p. 1354).

Locale-specific Discourses draw from larger, broader discourses but often represent localized adaptations that serve to regulate identity constructions in particular places. For example, in our own research, we found that the "ideal" high-tech entrepreneur identity was constructed uniquely in three different places (Gill & Larson 2014). Based on data that we gathered in different locations, we confirmed our assumptions that Silicon Valley represents a widely dispersed ideal for high-tech work, but also observed that this Discourse is adopted differently in unique locations. The Silicon Valley Discourse was largely replicated by entrepreneurs along the Wasatch front in Utah, but with a local twist related to cultural and religious norms of that population, such as more focus on family. On the other hand, in Missoula, Montana, local values related to "lifestyle" mixed with the Silicon Valley values to construct a very different idealized high-tech entrepreneur. For the Montana community, the ideal high-tech entrepreneur builds a business at the same time as enjoying local outdoor recreation opportunities. In fact, we found that the local norms themselves served to discipline self-identified entrepreneurs, as – in the case of Montana – there were social sanctions for working too hard and not living the local lifestyle. For people who want to identify as (high-tech) entrepreneurs, then, it is not only the Discourse of Silicon Valley that may discipline their identity, but locale-specific discourses may also influence how they narrate their identities, serving as forms of identity regulation.

Organizational Socialization and Culture Programs

Identity regulation is also produced through the creation of strong organizational cultures and the socialization of employees into those cultures. Cultural programs are widespread in modern organizations and these programs are, at least partially, about identity regulation. Starting with the turn toward organization culture in practice during the 1980s and inspired by best-selling management guru literature such as Deal and Kennedy's *Corporate Culture* (1988) and Peters and Waterman's *In Search of Excellence* (1982), managers began placing much more emphasis on shaping organizational culture as a way of manifesting organizational control. Attempts to construct "strong" cultures (see, e.g., Deal & Kennedy 1988) may be reframed as identity regulation because getting employees to buy into a culture influences how they will act and make decisions.

In a classic study of the culture of engineering (or, engineering culture), Kunda (1992) found that managers designed culture with the intent of regulating employees' hearts and minds. As a result, "full members" accepted the culture into their self-definition in order to be considered a successful organizational member and have better chances of moving up the organizational hierarchy. While not all members accepted the culture, the negative consequences of not doing so made identification with the organization attractive. The management-defined corporate culture functioned as a way to control identities because defining oneself, at least partially, according to that culture provided social status, economic rewards and positive identity reinforcement. The research on identity regulation, including concepts discussed previously in this chapter such as concertive control and self-discipline, therefore provide theoretical explanations for how strong cultures translate into control and high performance.

Rhetoric and Identification

At a more micro-level, rhetorical processes associated with identification provide explanation as to how normative control is produced. Because rhetoric and identification are discussed in detail in Chapter 3, this section will not explain how this process works, but rather demonstrate the ways in which persuasive communication is used to shape and regulate identities. In their discussion of identification as a tool for creating concertive control, Tompkins and Cheney (1985) assert that the traditional understanding of the rhetorical construct of the enthymeme does not go far enough in explaining how rhetoric is used in the service of control. In the traditional enthymeme, a speaker is persuasive because she or he draws on premises already held by the audience. For example, if you believe that protecting the environment is very important, then you are more likely to follow a course of action (such as recycling) recommended by a speaker who ties this to the value of protecting the environment.

Tompkins and Cheney (1985) argue, though, that persuasion in modern organizations often happens as the very values themselves are "inculcated" into the employees through communication processes. Here, inculcation refers to how an idea, value, or concept can be learned or internalized by hearing or experiencing it multiple times. The use of this word by Tompkins and Cheney is instructive for understanding how rhetoric works to create identity regulation. In enthymeme 2, the speaker persuades the audience to adopt actions based upon value premises that the speaker her or himself has persuaded the audience to adopt. To go back to our previous example about the environment, according to enthymeme 2, the speaker not only suggests a course of action (like recycling) but also inculcates the value of "care for the environment" into the audience (even, and especially, if the audience already held this value). Once the value premise is accepted, decision-making essentially becomes predetermined as people then go on to draw from these premises in making decisions (Simon 1976). There are many ways in which modern organizations seek to communicatively inculcate values into employees, including professional education programs, corporate culture programs and socialization practices. As employees identify with these value premises, accept them as their own and then draw upon these premises in order to make decisions, we see control over identity exercised. One recent scholarly example of how identity can be understood along these lines is in Wells (2013). Here, Wells applies enthymeme to her study of analytical chemists in the US, using it to demonstrate a disconnect between the idealized analytical chemist and the role experience of actual chemists. In doing this, she surfaces how value premises such as a preference for speaking "good" US-style English in the workplace shapes relations between highly skilled US-born and highly skilled foreign-born chemists, opportunities made available to foreign-born chemists and the identities of the foreign-born chemists themselves.

Resistance

Although most of this chapter focuses on identity regulation, it is certainly the case that individuals also resist such regulation. At the same time that they argue that identity regulation is real and widespread, most scholars also question the totality of managerial and organizational control over shaping and regulating identities. In Chapters 3 and 4, we stressed the agency of individuals to narrate and "work" on their identities, and characterized the identity work approach to research as tending toward agency (including resistance) rather than domination and control. For this next section on resistance, though, we focus on the ways in which control and resistance function in relation to one another, often in unpredictable and sometimes paradoxical ways.

Just as control in modern organizations is about identity, it makes sense that resistance should be, at least partially, about identity. So if control practices focus on producing individual identities in a certain way – possessing certain beliefs, values and ideologies – resistance practices reject that identity regulation and instead articulate alternative beliefs, values and ideologies. Identity regulation resistance may manifest in workers making fun of a new culture program when managers are not around, as an individual refuses to accept management's definition of who she or he is in the organization, as employees create websites to make fun of or parody the organization (Gossett & Kilker 2006), as employees refuse to take a work mentality into their home-lives or as employees publically demand concessions from management. In all of these instances, employees assert their own agency to narrate a sense of self in relationship to the discourses of identity regulation prescribed by the organization. Underlying all of these examples is the important recognition that identity regulation is always partial, conflicted and provides opportunities for resistance.

A Dialectic Approach to Control and Resistance

Harking back to our earlier discussion of Edwards' typologies of control and the dialectic of control, more specifically, we turn to Dennis Mumby's (1997; 2005) emphasis on a dialectical way of understanding control and resistance. Mumby had observed that previous research usually described control and resistance as an "either-or" situation, highlighting "(a) the practice of a wholly coherent, fully self-aware subject operating from a pristine, authentic space of resistance or (b) the activities of social actors that are subsumed within, and ultimately ineffectual against, a larger system of power relations" (Mumby 2005, p. 37). This parallels distinctions made in this book between identity work, which favors agency, and identity regulation, which favors control. Mumby suggests a dialectic approach as an alternative conceptualization that treats control and resistance as operating simultaneously and in relationship to each other. From this dialectical perspective, we can ask: how do individuals manage their identities when confronted with organizational efforts to monitor and control members? (Mumby 2005). Such an approach positions this agency and control dynamic as itself constitutive of identity formation and regulation.

A good example of the kind of dialectical analysis Mumby advocates is Kondo's (1990) study of gender, identity and work in a Japanese confectionary factory. Kondo examined the ways in which identity control was exerted not only by the factory management, but also by powerful cultural Discourses related to traditional gender roles in Japanese society. Her analysis demonstrates the complex relationship between control and resistance in regulating identities as the women asserted their status in the organization through identifying with and enacting maternal roles. Doing this provided a way for the women to assert a more esteemed cultural identity, but it also simultaneously disciplined them to traditional Japanese gender roles. Even Kondo herself struggled with these kinds of control and resistance identity issues during the year in which she was immersed in the organization and Japanese culture. At one notable moment, she walked by a shop window and saw her own reflection as a traditional Japanese woman and realized then that she had to leave before she "lost" her identity as an American researcher at a prestigious graduate program. The identity control was seductive as she found herself trying to fit into the culture she was studying. On the other hand, Kondo's decision to retreat from that context shows her own agency to make decisions to (re)construct her identity in alternative ways.

Overall, the dialectic approach to understanding identity control and resistance provides a useful conceptual framework for understanding the relationship between identity work and identity regulation. Most importantly, it stresses the need to always keep both of these opposing tensions in mind when analyzing identity. This does not only mean acknowledging that researchers might find greater evidence of control in some contexts and resistance in other contexts, but also being alert to the ways in which tensions and contradictions between control and resistance are managed simultaneously in everyday discursive practices.

Tensions, Ironies and Paradoxes of Control and Resistance

When researchers view control and resistance as in tension with each other, they often produce research findings that suggest ironic, contradictory and paradoxical outcomes of both control and resistance efforts. That is, efforts to control identities may actually produce resistance, and efforts to resist may actually reinstate control or conformity. Overt and sustained acts of resistance may reproduce systems of control and reinforce alienated identities (Willis 1977). Willis found this, for instance, in his study of working-class "lads" in Britain, where he questioned the cyclical nature of why young working-class men continued to get working-class jobs despite the availability of education and discourses of class mobility. In this classic text, Willis argued that resistance to education and class achievement paradoxically reproduced a kind of conformity amongst the working class that kept members of the working class within the socio-economic bracket. Similarly, Collinson (1988) illustrated how worker resistance to management control in the form of humor can ultimately reinscribe the subordinated position of workers. What this signals is that, although we often view identity regulation as something done by managers, and resistance as something done by employees, we cannot actually predict how Discursive control and resistance will manifest and develop within the discursive particulars of a given context, or over time.

A well-known study that demonstrates the contradictions in identity control and resistance comes from communication scholar Majia Holmer Nadesan. Holmer Nadesan (1996) studied female service workers in a graduate student housing facility at a mid-Western university in the United States. She found that management used identity regulation discourses related to patriarchy, bureaucracy and capitalism to construct the identities of the female service workers. For instance, in relation to gender, the women were positioned as subservient to male managers through such things as written rules that discouraged gossiping and that advised them to bathe regularly. In regard to capitalism and class, and despite official pronouncements otherwise, the managers informally framed the women as "peons" and "white trash." We can see how acceptance of such identity discourses would seem to make these women enact docile, subservient subject positions under the control of management. And yet, Holmer Nadesan argues that the women service workers expressed resistive, alternative identities in that they thought of themselves as "mothers away from home" or "second mothers" to the female graduate students living in the dorm. In doing this, these women crafted a much more appealing identity for themselves that tied into a culturally celebrated discourse of motherhood. Thus, on one hand, such resistance was successful in that the women found a "space for action" to reframe their identities in an alternative and more socially desirable way than what was offered by management. On the other hand, however, we can also see how the identity of "mothers away from home" reproduced management's notion of patriarchy, with the male managers positioned as the heads of the household. In addition, taking on such a motherhood role likely inspired the women to work harder, requiring a kind of self-discipline that ultimately benefitted management (as well as the graduate students). Overall, Holmer Nadesan shows not only the ways in which resistance to identity regulation is enacted, but also the ways in which the outcomes of resistance may be simultaneously resistive and controlling.

Meriläinen, Tienari, Thomas and Davies (2004) offer further lessons about the complexity and contradictions surrounding identity regulation and resistance. These researchers studied professional consultants and the ways in which they constructed their identities along the lines of a hyper-masculine discourse of "work addiction" and "self assertion" (p. 557), finding that this Discourse of management consultancy exerts considerable influence on identity construction, even across different cultural contexts. On the other hand, when the researchers looked at resistance discourse, such as those focused on work-life balance, they found differences in the two cultural contexts. In the UK, work-life balance discussions were viewed as resistant since they went against cultural norms that privileged work. In Finland, though, work-life balance discussions reinforced cultural norms and thus were not resistant discourses, but controlling ones. This study illuminates the shifting, complex relationship between control and resistance, where the same discourse might constitute resistance in one context and control in another.

Finally, a recent study of knowledge workers provides further lessons about the complexities and contradictions of understanding identity regulation in relationship to resistance. Costas and Kärreman (2016) found that managers created an appealing image of the management consultant that served as a force of identity regulation for employees. Here, management discourse presented the consultant as a creative, autonomous expert. In their day-to-day work life, though, some consultants expressed boredom, indicating that life as a knowledge worker was often routine, repetitive and mundane. Contrary to what we might expect, the authors argued that the "bored self" was not a kind of resistance, but rather a state of flux between what they hoped to become and the reality of daily work life, which they term an "arrested identity":

> An arrested identity is one where individuals are drained from drives to mobilize alternative selves and thus engage in resistance. This might add explanation to the lack of resistance noted in such work arrangements (Costas & Grey 2014; Kärreman & Alvesson 2009; Thornborrow & Brown 2009). The bored self arrests their identity as it implies that they still subscribe to the consulting dream, while enduring the disappointment of the work experience blaming the stupid work, and not themselves and their aspirations. (p. 77)

The idea of an arrested identity adds a new dimension to resistance, or rather the exercise of agency in pursuit of a preferred, if delayed, identity. The concept of an arrested identity likely tilts toward an identity regulation perspective, but does suggest another way in which agency is expressed in identity work.

Overall, there are not a lot of concrete predictions that scholars can make about control and resistance. Rather than this being a weakness of the theory, it reflects the complexities and specificities of identity work and identity regulation, and underscores the need to conduct careful analysis of situations before making pronouncements (which we discuss further in our final chapter). Although there are general influences that might make identity regulation more likely (e.g., strong, appealing organizational culture) or resistance more effective (e.g., support from colleagues or attractive alternatives) there is not a "magic list" of steps to creating identity regulation or resistance.

Disidentification

Another way to think about resistance is through the concept of disidentification. Where identification implies association, togetherness and forming linkages, "disidentification is associated with feelings of disconnection, separateness, and exclusion from the organization" (DiSanza & Bullis 1999, p. 380). Disidentification is very different from non-identification where someone does not form an association, but rather represents an active separation with an identity target (Pepper & Larson 2006). That is, disidentification implies forming an identity in opposition to a specific potential identification, or defining oneself by saying who you are not. For instance, in their study of this concept, Elsbach and Bhattacharya (2001) found that many people defined themselves in opposition to the National Rifle Association (NRA) in the United States. Participants in this research took pride in seeing their own beliefs and values as contrasted with those of the NRA. In this way, disidentification may thus function as a form of resistance to certain organizations and values.

To be sure, the NRA represents a fairly polarizing case in which to study issues of identification and disidentification. Researchers have nonetheless found disidentification to be in play in more "mundane" organizational situations, where employees may actively disidentify with the organization as a response to identity regulation. During a large corporate acquisition, Pepper and Larson (2006) found that attempts by the acquiring organization to socialize and assimilate employees were met with active disidentification from employees of the acquired organization. Actions that aimed to engender identification and commitment

120

were instead taken as evidence, by some participants, of a new divide between the organization and the individual. For example, when the acquiring company bought new computers for "incoming" employees, they gave the old, but almost new, computers they used previously to these employees to take home with them for personal use. For many people, this would be seen as an act of benevolence that could spark identification with the new/merged company. In this case though, employees from the acquiring organization saw it as an example of waste and inefficiency from a large, bureaucratic organization, and this way of thinking about the situation caused them to actively disidentify with the organization. In this, disidentification functioned as a form of resistance to attempts at identity regulation from the organization.

Identity, Materiality and Social Change

Our discussion thus far may raise questions about the extent to which identity control and resistance "matter" in our everyday lives. Although resistance to such control often manifests in one's ability to create an alternative identity, does this significantly make a difference in a person's life? In other words, does resistance to identity control produce meaningful, material changes? The ability to carve out an alternative workplace identity might provide for a more meaningful and socially validated sense of self, but does it lead to better pay or better physical working conditions? Communication scholar Dana Cloud (2001; 2005) stimulated conversations in organizational communication regarding the relationship between the material and the discursive worlds, including identity work/regulation. For Cloud, too much focus on the discursive aspects of organizational life ignores important material realities that are foundational for understanding the relationship between employees and managers. "Material realities" include such things as pay or other remuneration, working conditions, impact on the physical body and the work itself (e.g., tapping on a key board or making beds in a hotel). The discursive and the material worlds are intimately related, but too often since the discursive turn, organizational scholars have ignored the material and instead focused on the discursive (Aakhus et al. 2011; Cheney & Cloud 2006).

In particular, Cloud (2001) draws attention to social class (money/capital) as a primary organizing feature of everyday organizational life with potential for significant impact on the lives of employees. In critiquing trends related to the discursive approach, she stated:

> On the whole, however, emphasis in this literature remains on voice, identity, and cultural microstrategies in the workplace rather than on labor's agency in winning material improvements in the lives of workers. Class becomes one identity among others (rather than being formulated as a fundamental shared interest that enables solidarity across difference). (p. 269)

In a study of workplace labor unrest, Cloud (2005) found limitations in the power of rhetoric to shape the narratives of the workforce identity. In this labor dispute, Cloud noted a link between the workers' inability to enact material concessions from management and their changing discursive identity narratives:

> First, the workers' stories reveal the connection between the discursive constitution of identities and relationships on the one hand and the economic sources and resources that condition that discourse. Their shifts in self-narration, from warrior to victim to martyr, reflect their growing material powerlessness. Further, the stories and arguments of the workers show that lived experience of industrial (and other kinds of) work is a source of critical recognition of the need for redress beyond the symbolic. (Cloud 2005, p. 534)

Cloud reminds us that sometimes collective actions (e.g., forming a union or striking) are needed in addition to words to enact meaningful material resistance.

A related critique to Cloud's concerning the focus on discursive micro-strategies of resistance comes from Ganesh, Zoller and Cheney's (2005) article focusing on transformative resistance from below. For Ganesh et al., the focus on micro-strategies of resistance ignores potentially more important forms of resistance in contemporary society. Put differently, although scholars have focused on the resistive identity work in which individuals engage, they have largely missed careful analysis of collective, social movements that attempt to challenge traditional power structures and enact large-scale social changes. A widely cited example of such social movements is the 1999 protests in Seattle of the World Trade Organization (WTO) in which tens of thousands of protestors engaged in various acts of civil disobedience to disrupt the WTO meetings. Through such action, protesters found an effective way to voice resistance to globalization. This protest, and others, point to the potential impact of social movements to shape public understanding of key "big D" discourses like globalization.

Ganesh, Zoller and Cheney (2005) encouraged scholars to think beyond resistance as something that is engaged in by individuals in response to identity regulation. Rather, they suggest that collective resistance from below (from those less powerful – economically, socially and geographically) proffers greater possibilities for meaningful, transformative resistance. In terms of what this means for the study of identity regulation and resistance, this article points to the importance of seeing identity regulation and resistance as collective, including understanding how collective identities are shaped and what effects this has to create significant (material) changes. Individual (identity) resistance, unless linked with larger collective social movements, ultimately lacks real potential to create significant social change. A key area for future study therefore will be to translate how identity work at the individual level is linked to participation and organization of social movements. In other words, exploring the implications for and of identity as resistance efforts move from the individual to the collective.

More recent attention to the issue of materiality has seen discourse scholars unpacking and expanding the concept of materiality itself (see, e.g., *The Journal of Management Studies* forum on discourse and materiality, The Editors, 2015). Arguing that these "two phenomena are empirically distinct, but mutually implicated" (p. 706), Putnam (2015) advocates a dialectical view that "hold[s] the two in tension with one another, keep[s] them connected in continual interplay, and focus[es] on their co-emergence" (p. 707) as a way to avoid privileging one pole over the other. Other scholars have examined how the material design of technology and/or spaces are themselves driven by, and reproduce, entrenched discourses (Dean, Gill & Barbour 2016) or are overlaid with discourses that then inform material use and practice (Leonardi 2012). Certainly, the Communicative Constitution of Organization theory (Cooren 2004; Taylor & Van Every 2000) is entwined with attention to the material, as it examines the network of discursive and material influences within work- and organizationally related circumstances.

At a more micro- or individual level, discursive approaches to identity address the materiality of our bodies as a key factor in identity construction. Ashcraft (2007; 2013; Ashcraft & Mumby 2004) argues that the identities we derive from our work or occupations are inextricably linked to the bodies that have historically done this kind of work. As we have discussed in previous chapters, the "glass slipper" assumes that occupations have been constructed to "fit" certain bodies (and vice-versa), which means that our material "person" is keenly involved in identity construction. This has manifested in research that links the choices people make about dress and presentation to identity regulation (e.g., Alvesson 1994; Holmer Nadesan & Trethewey 2000). Turner and Norwood (2013), however, argue that bodies can themselves also be resistive in their study of how breastfeeding practices resist gendered and professionalized norms of the workplace.

Overall, the materialist critique of discursive identity research emphasizes important connections to make between the discursive and the material worlds, and the critique of individual resistance offers a critical reminder about the power of collective, social action. From our perspective, this is not to say that individual identity resistance to identity regulation is not meaningful or significant in the lives of employees. Rather, it is to emphasize that this is only part of the story. Identity work and identity regulation must be understood within the context of material and social influences that shape and are shaped by these processes.

Concluding Thoughts

This chapter focuses on identity as the modern contested terrain of contemporary control efforts in organizations. In many types of work, control is exercised by getting individuals to take on the values and beliefs of the organization and then adopt them as their own. Through various conceptualizations of normative control, scholars working from discursive approaches collectively construct an understanding of identity as influenced and produced by powerful discourses and interests. Although individuals have some agency to develop identities on their own, these choices are constrained by powerful organizations, appealing social identities and potent pressure from peers. To understand why people act the way they do is to investigate who they are and the forces that attempt to shape these identities.

Discussion Questions

1. What organizations have attempted to shape your identity? What are some messages you've heard that have been aimed at identity regulation? How successful has this identity regulation been?
2. Are regulatory or resistive discourses always "good" or "bad"? How can each enable or constrain identity construction and action in their own ways?
3. Which broad discourses in society are most powerful in regulating identities in contemporary society? Which discourses do you find yourself taking up? For example, do you take up the discourse of enterprise? What kinds of things might you or someone else say that indicate adherence to the discourse of enterprise?
4. In what ways do you resist identity regulation? What are specific things you do communicatively to disassociate yourself from particular identities?
5. Think of the place where you work, volunteer or study. How does the physical layout of this place enable (or dissuade) particular kinds of action? Does the physical layout help with getting tasks done, or

hinder tasks? Do the kinds of communication fostered by the physical layout align with what you think communication *should* look like regarding that occupation, career or organization type? Why or why not?

6

Informing Key Organizational Processes through Discursive Approaches to Identity

Six months into a major acquisition at TechCo and things were not going well. Joe, the human resource manager, wondered what had gone so wrong. TechCo had purchased a competitor, a startup called CIE, for three hundred million dollars, with the intent of capitalizing on CIE's inventions and complementing products already in the TechCo line. On paper, the TechCo and CIE product lines looked like a perfect match. Unfortunately, the cultures of the two companies were very different. As a Fortune 500 company, TechCo was large and stable and had a "northern-California"-inspired commitment to participative decision-making. CIE, on the other hand, was a relatively young company with a do-or-die attitude shaped by its struggles to compete in a fast-changing environment.

Upon acquisition, the CIE employees became TechCo employees, but stayed at their previous work sites and so remained physically isolated. The new, merged company now included former TechCo work sites in California and Washington, as well as the new CIE sites in Chicago and Florida. In order to make this combined organization work, TechCo managers knew they had to rely on information communication technologies (ICTs). Workers from the various sites would not have the luxury of even meeting most of their co-workers face-to-face and visits by senior managers were infrequent. As a result, Joe and the general manager devised a plan to build a cohesive organizational culture, socialize employees and create organizational identification using mediated communication. For starters, they implemented a monthly online town hall meeting where participants used a combination of internet and conference-calling technologies to meet together. These online town hall meetings included updates from managers as well as time to answer questions from workers across the sites. In addition, the GM and HR directors held weekly online office hours where they could answer questions and help employees negotiate changes resulting from the merger. Finally, the company set up an online messaging system so that employees could be in easy contact with co-workers at various sites.

From Joe's perspective, however, the online town hall meetings and other efforts to build a cohesive culture seemed to be having the opposite effect. Ex-CIE employees had identified strongly with their old CIE culture, and they were beginning to articulate identities that were in opposition to the TechCo organization. The ICTs played a particular role in this, as they became symbolic of all the CIE employees disliked about the new organization. That is, ICT use actually fostered disidentification from CIE employees as they associated online town hall meetings with an impersonal, bureaucratic and distant organization (Sitkin, Sutcliffe & Barrios-Choplin 1992).

This example of the TechCo-CIE merger demonstrates how identity intersects with key processes and problems studied by scholars of organizations. In this example, the study of ICTs is linked to how organization members conducted identity work, including the formation of disidentifications that themselves were associated with the symbolic construction of ICTs as undesirable. In this chapter, we draw connections between the discursive approach to organizations and identity, and fundamental organizational constructs including technology, leadership, decision-making and socialization. Intersections among conceptual interests such as these have the potential to inform both research on identity as well as research on these topics themselves.

Technology and Identity

One of the most prominent overlaps with discursive organizations and identity research comes from the study of ICTs, which
is why we began this chapter with the example of the TechCo-CIE
merger. In a lot of ways this overlap makes sense: organizations
increasingly rely on ICTs, and scholars continue to ask how the
use of them influences other processes like identity formation.
Three main themes connect to the discursive construction of
identity in this research literature: identification in virtual teams;
the symbolic shaping of technology and identity; and identity and
technology workers.

Identification in Virtual Teams

The most common theme in research linking identity and technology involves studying the organizational use of virtual groups
or teams. This research typically explores ICTs as mediating the
relationship between the individual and the organization, and
attempts to understand what impacts ICT use has on member
identification with the organization. Important questions include:
How does the use of ICTs influence member identification with
the overall organization or with a sub-group? Do different types of
ICTs influence identification differently? How do different imple-
mentations and uses of ICTs influence identification? Although
the research findings have some variability, there are some trends
across this literature that we can point out.

Research from the SIT tradition accounts for a significant
number of identity/technology related research in the area of
online groups. One SIT-related research program, called social
identity/deindividuation (SIDE) theory, focuses on how CMC
(computer mediated communication) provides some cues for
group identity formation while also filtering out other cues, like
nonverbal communication (Postmes, Spears & Lea 1998; 2000;
Scott 2007; Walther & Parks 2002). In general, findings from
SIDE theory suggest that individuals develop stronger group or

social identifications when certain individual cues, like appearance, are filtered out because of CMC. This is because in CMC groups, users tend to overemphasize perceived commonalities as evidence of social similarity when faced with a lack of information that might otherwise individualize each user.

For example, if you join an online support group for cancer survivors, you are likely to identify more strongly with the group and perceive more similarities with other members because of your shared experience than if you met face-to-face. The lack of knowledge about specific individuals heightens the importance of other, often self-selected, characteristics (such as that around a particular interest or experience) that guide decision-making around whether or not to associate or disassociate with a group. For instance, think about the social media feeds or sites that you have voluntarily joined, friended or liked. Your choice to follow a particular Tumblr or subscribe to a group or organization's Instagram is often driven by a similarity that you perceive between the media feed and its members and yourself, even though you would likely find that a number of dissimilarities exist if you were to meet the other subscribers. Ultimately, it seems that we see ourselves as more similar to and, thus, more connected with others in a self-selected group if we know less about the diverse nature of others, rather than more.

SIDE research attempts to tease out the conditions that lead to lesser or greater identification with the group. For instance, Scott's (1999) study utilizing SIDE found that discursive anonymity (where participants did not know who made certain comments) led to greater group identification than other types of anonymity. Overall, SIDE research points to profound ways in which communication mediums may alter identification processes, including the counterintuitive, specific finding that less information might lead to stronger identification in certain contexts. On the other hand, this research tends to focus on lab-based, manipulated experiments, so the generalizability of the findings to naturally occurring groups and groups with prior interaction history in organization contexts is uncertain (Scott 2007; Walther & Parks 2002).

Other approaches to studying ICTs and identity address SIT and the ways in which technologically mediated communication influences identity formations. Here, some SIT research draws from an understanding of media richness theory, positing communication mediums as lean or rich. Through this lens, richer media are seen to carry more communication cues, offer immediate feedback, personalize messages and use natural language (Daft & Lengel 1984; 1986). For instance, face-to-face communication is often described as the most "rich" communication medium as it has the ability to transfer lots of different cues (i.e., nonverbal) in addition to offering immediate feedback and personalized and conversational language. A key assumption of media richness theory is that richer media are needed to communicate more complex and ambiguous information, although some studies of CMC have found exceptions (Walther & Parks 2002).

Yet, at the same time that SIT studies of identification and technology find that richer media enable organizational identification, they also find that lean media better foster group identification than *moderately rich* media (Pratt 2001; Rock & Pratt 2002). This means that the richness of the media may impact the likelihood of forming or not forming identification, though there is much going on that still needs to be discovered. In a review of research on identification and CMC from the SIT perspective, Scott (2007) concludes:

> With virtual workers using communication technologies, we have probably been overly reliant on somewhat suspect media richness explanations, and we seem far from grasping the interactions of virtuality, telepresence, and identification that a social-identity based view of such work demands. In sum, the existing work suggests that examining identity creation and strength of identification issues during computer-mediated communication is clearly warranted, but that work has only just started in traditional and virtual organizational settings. (p. 129)

As an example of SIT research that links identification and technology, Scott and Timmerman (1999) studied teleworkers using ICTs and found the strongest connection between organizational identification and moderate use of ICTs. In addition, they found that the use of advanced technologies like audio conferencing and cell phone use were most associated with strong identification. These findings usefully point to the non-linear relationship between ICTs and identification (i.e., more usage does not necessarily mean stronger identification) and the ways in which different types of ICTs may or may not foster identification. The researchers also hinted at the complexity of such relationships when they speculate that one of the reasons for a strong correlation between identification and use of audio conferencing is that the folks using such conferencing technologies were already likely to be highly involved in the organization. Interestingly, they ventured that those using cell phones might indicate stronger identification because they felt special for being given such advanced technologies to use. Yet, in today's world, because cell phones are no longer considered "advanced technology" in many professional or corporate organizations, the likelihood that employees would feel special because they had been given such technology is less, and so this finding highlights the changing nature of the relationship between ICT use and identification. Although beyond the scope of this chapter, a number of other studies have also explored the implications of telecommuting and virtual teams on organizational identification from a SIT perspective (Sohrabi, Gholipour & Amiri 2012; Thatcher & Zue 2006).

The Symbolic Shaping of Technology and Identity

The variability in the findings from the virtual teams research discussed in the previous section suggests that it is difficult to capture the complexities of identity formation in the context of ICT use. In this section, we therefore examine research that takes more of a discursive approach to understanding both technology and identity that sheds light on how communication technologies and identities are mutually constructed. From this perspective, communication technologies may shape how identity work is accomplished and vice-versa – identities may shape the ways in which communication technologies are used and understood. As is discussed in the framework of this book, researchers tend to tilt toward explanations for social phenomena that favor either agency or structure. In the technology literature, there is a similar debate as to how to balance interpretations highlighting technological determinism (understood as where the technology itself determines how ICTs are adopted) and interpretations highlighting social factors (understood as where social constructions shape the adoption and use of technologies) (Jackson, Poole & Kuhn 2002). It is worth keeping this tension in mind as we discuss some examples of research from a more discursive perspective.

ICTs influence people to pay attention to different types of information, and this may have implications for identity work. This process is additionally mediated by relations of power, in that it is often advantageous for one party to determine the technology that will be used, so as to have a hand in shaping the information that will rise to the surface or be given more attention. For example, Coombs, Knights and Willmott (1992) found that the UK National Health Service made financial information available to doctors via particular communication technologies in order to make doctors pay more attention to medical costs. By having this financial information readily available, doctors were also encouraged to construct their professional identities in different ways. As Coombs et al. (1992) suggest, the use of technology supports ". . . the creation of specific information systems which privilege particular kinds of information and reinforce certain forms of knowledge about what the N.H.S. is, and what doctors are and what their goals and procedures should be" (p. 68). Specifically, the communication of financial information contributed to doctors seeing themselves as managers of budgets which might, subsequently, cause them to pay even more attention to financial information. Thus, this example demonstrates how the ability of hospital administrators to control the information that is seen or unseen through ICTs influences identity work. The researchers point to the "value of a theory of power and subjectivity as a means of understanding the dynamics of the practices through which the presence and power of I.C.T.s is interpreted, supported, resisted and refined" (p. 69).

A more recent study that demonstrates the promise of the

discursive identity lens for communication technologies is Nelson and Irwin's (2014) study of how librarians negotiated their occupational identities (as experts in finding information) in response to the rise of Internet search engines. The authors found a reciprocal relationship here: not only did the occupational identities of librarians influence how they interpreted and interacted with the Internet, but the Internet then influenced how they (re)formulated their occupational identities. Many librarians initially resisted the use of the Internet because it challenged the expert identities they had built up. And, their perception of the Internet as a threat to this identity influenced the adoption (or lack of adoption) of Internet searching. Nelson and Irwin found that, as a result, librarians missed opportunities to shape this technology to better innovate library research. Yet, after the Internet became established as the place to find information (despite the resistance), librarians reframed their occupational identities in relationship to the Internet, by redefining librarians as teachers of Internet search (i.e., helping others find their own information) and as connectors of people with information. In addition, this reformulation of occupational identity actually led librarians to engage with the technology developers to create better Internet search resources for libraries. Overall, this study shows the multi-directional relationship between the social construction of identity and technology and suggests further study is necessary to explicate this relationship.

A rhetorical lens further helps explain the mutually constructed relationship between identity and technology. Symon (2008) found that identity construction can function as a rhetorical strategy during a period of technological change in an organization, demonstrating that the success or failure of a technology is, in part, predicated on the rhetorical moves of organizational participants. That is, by framing technologies and the people associated with them as competent or incompetent, rhetors shape whether a technology is accepted or rejected, as well as the identities of those connected with that technology. Specifically, in Symon's study, the rhetorical construction of IT staff as incompetent served both to discredit a technology change initiative and to frame the identities of the IT staff in a particular way for political purposes. Symon (2008) stresses that the "constructing of identities is a rhetorical strategy" (p. 94) used to shape not only identities, but also the technology itself. The rhetorical lens usefully demonstrates how social constructions, of both technologies and identities, are often strategic and political.

Identity and Technology Workers

A third area where discursive approaches to organizations and identity overlap with research on ICTs focuses on high-tech or knowledge workers. More and more, the engineers, technicians, and scientists who design technologies form a large and influential group of workers in contemporary society. Scholars have asserted that while the lives and needs of this relatively privileged group of workers may not invoke much social sympathy, this group deserves attention because they represent the future of a particular form of work (creative class or knowledge work) and hold significant social and political influence in society (Deetz 1998). In particular, technology workers may epitomize a workforce disciplined through identity work and regulation.

In the classic study of the culture of an engineering organization discussed previously, Kunda (1992) showed that culture served as a form of controlling employees. In an in-depth, ethnographic study of one high-tech company, Kunda found that the culture of the organization influenced how individual employees constructed their identities. Overall, Kunda's research provides evidence, confirmed by many subsequent studies, that control of knowledge work happens through the shaping of professional, occupational and organizational identities.

Although an overview of the research on the discipline of technology workers through identity control is beyond the scope of this chapter (we also discussed this, to some degree, in Chapter 5), there exists a strong research connection between identity and the control of knowledge work. For example, Jian (2008) found that a "technologist" identity among workers at a campus IT services organization served as a way for workers to resist managers, but also as a powerful form of self-discipline. Larson and Pepper (2003) found that aerospace workers were controlled and constrained through identification with company values. Wieland (2010) found that constructions of ideal selves served to discipline employees in a multinational research and development organization, and Deetz (1998) discovered that employees in a tele-communications company constructed their identities as internal "consultants" which led to substantial self-discipline in the service of customer and organizational objectives. Taken together, these studies (and many others) provide a clear link between technology and/or knowledge work and the regulation and work of identity.

Leadership and Identity

Another key intersection of identity and organization research can be found in the study of leadership. Leadership remains one of the most popular topics of analysis amongst both organizational researchers and practitioners. A quick search for books on Amazon.com for leadership reveals over 180,000 results with over 1,000 books released in just the last 30 days. A Google Scholar search of academic texts with the word "leadership" in the title returned 223,000 results with 992 results in just the first three months of 2016. Although certainly a rough gauge, this survey of recent publications demonstrates the enduring interest and applicability of leadership as an important topic in contemporary society. The following section explores how an identity lens on leadership can help scholars and practitioners to better understand leadership processes.

A Discursive Perspective on Leadership and Identity

Much of the popular understanding of and research on leadership conceptualizes leadership from a psychological lens. As with studies of identity and organizations, a psychological lens is useful for understanding certain aspects of leadership, but perhaps not others. A psychological view of leadership tends to focus attention on such things as cognitive processes, individuals as opposed to collectives, leadership as an "essence," and communication as secondary (Fairhurst 2007). A discursive approach, on the other hand, is more likely to direct attention to the social construction of meanings, collectives rather than individuals, decentered subjects, and communication as primary (see Fairhurst 2007 for a comprehensive review of these traditions). Although both psychological and discursive approaches have strengths and weaknesses for understanding leadership, we would agree with the argument made by Gail Fairhurst (2007) that a discursive approach generates a more comprehensive understanding of leadership, including in the relationship between identity and leadership.

To get a sense of the self as described in leadership psychology, it is worth briefly exploring two popular psychology-based theories on leadership and identity (Fairhurst 2007): follower self-identity theory (Lord & Brown 2004) and authentic leadership (Avolio & Gardner 2005). Follower self-identity theory asserts that a primary function of leadership is to shape the way followers feel about themselves to elicit improved organizational performance. Authentic leadership theory, drawing from a movement called positive psychology, posits that leaders should get in touch with their real selves or true selves. Here, Avolio and Gardner (2005) forward the premise that, "through increased self-awareness, self-regulation, and positive modeling, authentic leaders foster the development of authenticity in followers. In turn, followers' authenticity contributes to their well-being and the attainment of sustainable and veritable performance" (p. 317). As this demonstrates, the authentic leadership approach assumes that individuals have a true self that can be found and that, once found, the true self will lead to greater satisfaction and productivity. This true self is grounded in the Western belief in the individual as a separate, unique, and integrated whole.

In contrast to authentic leadership theory, discursive approaches to leadership suggest that people have multiple identities and that none of these is the one true identity. Similar to the real-self↔ fake-self dichotomy (Tracy & Trethewey 2005) discussed in Chapter 4, the assertion that individuals have multiple identities is a useful way for both scholars and practitioners to conceive of identity and leadership. For scholars, this centers attention on the management of multiple identities, arguably the most important identity-related practice in contemporary society, whereas practitioners recognize how the real-self↔fake-self dichotomy produces stress and anxiety as individuals search for a true self that is ultimately elusive. This is not to say that from a discursive perspective leadership identity is completely contradictory and fragmented. Rather, individuals must weave different identity narratives together in an ongoing process of identity construction. In a study of authentic leadership from a discursive perspective, for example, Nyberg and Sveningsson (2014) found that authentic leadership was socially constructed within local contexts by managers. Specifically, they found that although managers wanted to engage in "heroic" (read: individualized) leadership behaviors, the realities of local situations often required them to be more participative in their leadership actions. To reconcile this tension, managers used metaphors (Mother Theresa, messiah, and coach) to manage their competing identities in such a way that allowed them to adjust to situational demands of leadership that required participative forms of leadership, while still allowing them to hold onto a socially constructed "authentic" self. What this study shows is that although there is popular appeal to create an authentic self, doing so involves active management of paradoxes and takes considerable, ongoing identity work in order to narrate a leadership identity.

Identity Regulation and Leadership

We distinguished between identity work and identity regulation in previous chapters. This distinction is also useful in considering the contributions a discursive approach to identity can make to the literature on leadership. In particular, the identity regulation lens highlights how leadership discourses shape contemporary notions of leaders, and the identity work lens highlights the ways in which individuals navigate multiple leadership discourses to narrate unique identities. This section explores identity regulation to better understand leadership and identity.

Much of the research from a discursive approach adopts an identity regulation lens when examining leadership. Remember, scholars that tilt toward an identity regulation perspective look to the ways in which Discourses produce identities. Often drawing from Foucault, much of this research focuses on how contemporary notions of who leaders are and what they do are used in the service of control in organizations. Think about the leadership industry (remember all those books on leadership that we found by searching Amazon.com and Google Scholar!) that provides all sorts of advice on what the ideal leader should be like. These leadership discourses construct leader-identities that good/effective managers are expected to follow. So rather than thinking of leadership as something that is inside the person waiting to be discovered, a discursive approach articulates leadership as instead existing in the external discourses that people take up to define themselves as leaders. When particular leadership discourses gain currency in managerial discourse, managers are encouraged (by the Discourse, including through mentors or employers, University or training courses, and popular and scholarly press books) to adopt those discourses or to risk being seen as out-of-touch. Consider the specific concept of "authentic" leadership from a discursive perspective.

From a discursive perspective, "authentic leadership" may be thought of as a construction designed to regulate managers' thoughts and behaviors in ways that benefit the organization. When individuals buy into the idea that there really is something that is "authentic leadership" and discipline themselves in order to enact this identity, they are effectively controlled through this discourse. We see an example of this in a study by Costas and Fleming (2009) where an employee named Paul struggled to affiliate what he saw as his authentic sense of self with the identity "designed" by the corporation for which he worked. Costas and Fleming observed that Paul found it "increasingly difficult to define himself via his narrated imaginary of authenticity (as an intellectual, musician and creative type who is attracted to countercultural issues) and thus [began] to experience himself as a reflection of an alien corporate identity (Costas & Fleming 2009, p. 368). Based on their findings, Costas and Fleming suggest that leadership authenticity is a "narrated imaginary" in which the authentic self is narrated (i.e., imagined) in opposition to the preferred, designed self of the corporation (p. 354). Rather than existing as a true self to be discovered, instead these authors frame the leadership identity as a socially constructed ideal self that is articulated in comparison to a compromised self at work. This means that the authentic self is a contested discursive construction, instead of a virtuous inner self.

Yet, the popular leadership literature undoubtedly extolls the ideal, authentic inner self. Although there are subtle variations, the ideal authentic leader embodies similar traits across many discourses. Gardner, Avolio, Luthans, May and Walumbwa (2005) suggest that the:

> [A]uthentic leader must achieve authenticity ... through self awareness, self-acceptance, and authentic actions and relationships. However, authentic leadership extends beyond the authenticity of the leader as a person to encompass authentic relations with followers and associates. These relationships are characterized by: (a) transparency, openness, and trust, (b) guidance toward worthy objectives, and (c) an emphasis on follower development. (p. 345)

As a discourse that prescribes and privileges certain characteristics, behaviors and identities over others, authentic leadership may be conceived as a normative form of control that attempts to shape leaders into a particular framework. If one accepts authentic leaders according to this framework, and strives to achieve such an identity, then this Discourse plays a role in regulating identity. But what happens when one's authentic self does not align with the organizationally or socially desired self? What we see here is a Discourse that instructs leaders to *be themselves*, and yet also presupposes that there is a "right" self to be.

A discursive approach therefore critiques the authentic leadership paradigm for categorizing sanctioned, positive traits as "authentic" and negative traits as "inauthentic." Leadership discourses instruct people to find an inner self that is virtuous, self-aware and highly regulated. Leaders who act in other ways have supposedly not yet found or tapped into their authentic selves. In this, the authentic self Discourse is convenient because it provides a way for leaders to reject responsibility for "bad" decisions they must make as "not theirs," and take pride in "good" decisions they make as guided by their virtuous, true self. In exploring this, Gail Fairhurst (2007) cites the example of Linda Wachner, a CEO and one of "America's Toughest Bosses," to demonstrate how authentic leadership discourses get enacted. We could ask if Wachner – an aggressive boss who often yells at employees – lacks awareness of a virtuous inner self (i.e., she has not yet found her authentic self) or if these negative traits represent Wachner's authentic self (i.e., she has found her authentic self and it is aggressive and lacks self awareness). A discursive perspective answers this question according to the worldview of the interpreter. As Fairhurst (2007) argued, "... each Discourse produces its own truth effects by portraying certain traits and behaviors as authentic and others as inauthentic" (p. 104). A discursive identity perspective on leadership is thus useful for drawing attention to the ways in which authenticity and inauthenticity are socially constructed and contextually situated.

Another popular trend in the leadership literature, "transformational leadership," which, notably, distinguishes between the roles of "manager" and "leader," is also usefully understood from a discursive identity perspective. The manager/leader distinction positions managers as overseeing daily operations and transformational leaders as change agents who manage meanings and identities in organizations (Bryman, 1996). This Discourse describes leaders as "transformational" figures who embody the more desirable traits that good, successful leaders should emulate as opposed to managers who simply maintain the status quo. From a discursive perspective, this distinction is a socially constructed norm meant to celebrate and encourage certain types of identities and actions as constituting leadership and other, less desirable identities and activities as constituting management. Similar to the authentic leader, the transformational leader represents a Discourse that serves as a resource for narrating and regulating identities in organizations.

Another way to see leadership as identity regulation stems

from the ways in which leadership Discourse is underpinned and entwined with assumptions about gender, race/ethnicity and class. That is, the image of the leader that emerges in much of the mainstream leadership discourse is often that of the white, upper-middle class (or otherwise privileged) male. Even in contexts where gender is explicitly taken into account, such as in studies of women and leadership, the dominant Discourse favors and is predicated on the experiences of white women of privilege. In her book, *Race, Gender and Leadership*, Patricia Parker (2005) critiques what is known as the "female advantage" model of leadership, noting that this model articulates women as having a unique advantage over men in the area of leadership because they possess inherent traits such as cooperation. Parker keenly notes, however, that this model excludes the narratives and experiences of African American women leaders, observing that "Contemporary African American women's organizational leadership is grounded in a tradition of survival, resistance and change that, historically, has been ignored or devalued" (p. xiv). As a result, the discourses that frame successful leadership, and successful women's leadership in this case, narrate an identity that is inaccessible to many individuals in society from diverse backgrounds.

The entwining of social identity in leadership Discourses functions as a form of identity regulation because it promotes leadership among people who "naturally" look or act the part, and restricts access to leadership by people who do not. It furthermore encourages comportment to the ideal, amongst all people who identify as (or want to identify as) leaders. This is not to say that alternative narratives of leader identity do not exist, although we would note that they struggle to gain traction in popular leadership discourses. An example of this is articulated by Parker (2005), where she found that African American women executives constructed an understanding of leadership as a *combination of confrontation and collaboration* so as to redefine traditional masculine/feminine leadership distinctions that did not otherwise "speak" to them. Here, the executives used a mix of confrontational voice and collaborative voice, depending on the context. This articulation of leadership represents an alternative conception of what a good or successful leadership identity should look like, although, as Parker notes, it has struggled to be recognized given the hegemonic power of traditional leadership discourses. From a discursive leadership perspective, this study again points to the ways in which leadership identity is a contested, narrated discourse that regulates identities.

Finally, one more example demonstrates the ways in which leadership is usefully constructed through an identity regulation lens and also points to some limitations of this lens. Gagnon (2008) examined corporate management training programs at two companies and found evidence that both these programs were identity regulation programs that compelled organization members to engage in internal identity work and external positioning to take up the prescribed training program identities. While Gagnon found evidence of these management training programs leading to identity regulation from participants, he also found variations in the degree of control exercised in the two organizations. Utilizing Collinson's (2003) notion of identity insecurity, Gagnon shows how participants in the training programs varied their responses to the identity regulation program. At one organization, which had high levels of symbolic and material insecurity, Gagnon found that identities were more tightly regulated through the training program. In the other company, with less insecurity, the responses of individuals, while controlled in some ways, were more varied and more resistive. Thus, although leadership discourses may be initially conceptualized as regulating identity, it is important to recognize that the responses of individuals to such discourses are varied, even resistive, and that people draw from an array of (alternative) discourses to construct a leadership identity.

Identity Work and Leadership

Although much of the research on leadership and identity focuses on leadership as identity regulation, a smaller number of scholars have focused on leadership from an identity work perspective. As discussed in Chapter 3, identity work tilts toward the agency of individuals to narrate and construct their own identities by drawing upon a wide variety of available discursive resources.

Remember, few if any scholars would argue that people are completely free to construct their identities in any way they choose, but identity work scholars tend to emphasize individual agency in this process. Identity work provides a useful lens to conceptualize the processes taking place during leadership development.

An identity work approach to leadership suggests that individuals negotiate multiple identity discourses during the process of becoming a leader and assuming a leadership identity. In addition, this leadership identity is an ongoing construction that is continually negotiated and renegotiated as individuals engage new experiences and reflect on the communicated interpretations of others. This perspective is conceptually predicated on the notion that a "space of action" (Holmer Nadesan 1996) always exists in which people have the ability to make their own decisions among competing discursive alternatives. Even when leadership discourses are strongly prescribed, like we discussed in the "authentic leadership" discourse, individuals may draw upon competing and alternative discourses to narrate their own leadership identities.

In a study utilizing the space of action concept, Carroll and Levy (2010) found that leaders utilized different identity work strategies during a leadership development program. Despite that the program prescribed a narrow sense of who leaders should be, these participants drew on alternative discourses of leadership, as well as other discourses about themselves, to create unique leader identities. Specifically, Carroll and Levy pointed to three ways that participants negotiated the organizational efforts to shape identities: assimilation, complementarity, and rejection, which encompass a range from highly regulated (assimilation) to highly resistive (rejection). Taken together, these different responses indicate the variety of possible outcomes of identity work undertaken in the face of organizationally sanctioned leadership discourses. Furthermore, Carroll and Levy (2010) suggest that leadership development involves identity work that includes "the creation and sustaining of multiple discursive fields where identities inevitably compete, struggle, contradict, lure, seduce, repel, dominate, and surprise" (p. 225). These scholars do not deny that some discourses are more appealing and, thus, controlling than others, but rather indicate that despite pressures to conform, individuals possess some semblance of agency to choose from among a range of discursive resources.

An identity work perspective on leadership thus provides an alternative to thinking about leadership as specific traits that leaders embody and instead forces attention on the ongoing storytelling process where people (re)negotiate what it means to be a leader. This shifts attention to leadership as socially constructed and suggests that "leadership" is not one thing, but rather is many different possibilities constructed individually and socially in unique contexts. An identity work perspective suggests that the storytellers have at least some agency in shaping their own stories, but the stories that leaders tell are also best understood in the context of other, ongoing and changing stories. This reminds us that identity work and identity regulation are best understood in relationship to each other. A recent article in *The New Yorker* (Rotham 2016) eloquently frames how leadership identities emerge and change:

> To some extent, leaders are storytellers; really, though, they are characters in stories. They play leading roles, but in dramas they can't predict and don't always understand. Because the serialized drama of history is bigger than any one character's arc, leaders can't guarantee our ultimate narrative satisfaction. Because events, on the whole, are more protean than people, leaders grow less satisfying with time, as the stories they're ready to tell diverge from the stories we want to hear. And, because our desire for a coherent vision of the world is bottomless, our hunger for leadership is insatiable, too. Leaders make the world more sensible, but never sensible enough. (para. 29)

Identity work constitutes at least part of current conceptualizations of leadership and serves as a lens for understanding this process.

Although this section makes an argument that identity functions as a useful lens for understanding contemporary notions of leadership, leadership is not only about identity. Leadership consists of a variety of processes and activities that have more or less to do with identity regulation and identity work. Sorting through the activities that create and reinforce a particular identity takes careful analysis. Say, for instance, a student reserves a room for her study group to meet. We could say that this is leadership behavior, but also that it does not necessarily influence how she constructs her identity narrative. On the other hand, if others recognize this activity as leadership and communicate their understanding of it as leadership to her, then it might become part of her identity narrative. Our point is that identity provides a lens to better understand leadership processes, and likely an underutilized one, but we also do not claim that leadership is completely understood through any one analytical lens.

Identity and Organizations: Connections with other Research

The previous two sections, on technology and leadership, demonstrate the utility of an identity lens for understanding organizational processes. This section offers brief summaries of several other key areas of research overlap including decision-making, socialization and place.

Decision-making

In the field of organization studies, decision-making is one of the most studied topics, and identity and identification significantly influence organizational decision-making. One of the first definitions of organizational identification, from Herbert Simon (1976), directly links these concepts: "A person identifies with a group when, in making a decision, he [sic] evaluates the several alternatives of choice in terms of the consequences for the specified group" (p. 205). Simon asserts that the fundamental building block of decision-making is the "premise." Decision premises, including values, beliefs and facts, shape the outcomes of decisions. For Simon, if the decision premises of individuals can be shaped, then their decision-making becomes predictable, or even "predetermined." In this way, the identifications that people form, and the subsequent incorporation of those identifications into aspects of ones identity, regulate decision-making. For example, if a lawyer accepts the premise that all clients deserve spirited representation, then that lawyer will most likely engage in that type of representation, even in the face of an unpleasant or despicable client. Decisions flow from the premises we hold, but there are often many, at times competing, premises that influence any one decision. It is not always easy to say which premises are most influential in which decisions.

The research on identity and control also assumes a link between identity and organizational decision-making. Identity regulation functions as organizational control due to a perceived link between "who am I?" and "how should I act?". That is, in influencing identity construction, organizations also influence the decisions made by employees – ideally with the best interests of the organization in mind. Because identity regulation is explored in detail in Chapter 5, we won't go into depth here except to highlight this connection between decision-making, control and identity.

A key critique of Simon's (1976) link between identification and decision-making centers on assumptions made by Simon about the rationality of actors. Although we might rationally expect human actors to make decisions consistent with their value premises, sometimes individuals make decisions that seemingly go against premises that they hold closely. Other factors, like emotions or peer pressure, also shape the decisions that humans make. In addition, scholars have demonstrated that the appearance of rationality is more important in many contexts than actual rational decision-making. For example, Karl Weick's (1995) work on sense-making suggests that actors make sense of their actions retrospectively and assign meaning to those actions based on the outcomes – a process that is antithetical to the rational model of decision-making. So while identity and identification clearly influence decision-making, it is not enough to simply understand one's decision premises, as the decision-making process is more complex. As anyone knows who has ever made a decision of which they are ashamed, sometimes we act in ways that are not consistent with who we think we are.

Socialization

Identity and identification studies inform and are informed by research on organizational socialization. Socialization research examines the ways in which organization members enter new organizations and become members of those organizations. Socialization, interchangeable or closely related conceptually to assimilation, represents a key process in organizational entry and exit that has implications for understanding organizations and identity.

Researchers typically divide the socialization process into four stages that begin prior to entering the organization and conclude after the individual exits the organization. Synthesizing previous research, Kramer (2010) summarizes four stages of socialization: anticipatory socialization, encounter, metamorphosis/role management, and exit. *Anticipatory* socialization includes processes that occur prior to even encountering a particular workplace and include vocational anticipatory socialization (choosing what one wants to do for work or an occupation) and organizational anticipatory socialization (choosing a specific organization) (Jablin 2001). From a very young age, most of us engage in conversations about "what we might want to do when we grow up." Choosing a college major in modern society often involves choices related to future work (see Lair & Wieland 2012). In addition, after we've chosen a particular vocational path, we also make assumptions about particular organizations based on the following types of questions: Is this a good place to work? Does it share the same values that I do? What do others think of this organization? Will it provide opportunities for growth?

The next stage in the socialization process is *encounter*, where the individual enters the organization as a newcomer and begins to learn new organizational roles. The encounter period is marked by experiences that confirm and/or challenge previous expectations about the organization. From there is *metamorphosis/role management* where individuals transition from newcomers to full-fledged members of the organization (Kramer 2010). During this stage, members negotiate and adapt their roles to eventually find their fit within the organization. The final stage in assimilation, *exit*, consists of leaving the organization either voluntarily or involuntarily. Just like in the other phases, exit requires considerable sense-making from individuals.

Each of the stages of organizational socialization links closely with identification and identity. For instance, in *anticipatory socialization*, our understanding of organizations and our perceptions of compatibility are linked to our identities and previous experiences. One's occupational and personal identities will shape how one perceives a job offer from a particular organization, for instance. Consider how a law student might struggle with an offer from a large corporation, say a soft drink company like Pepsi or Coke, because the company's products might conflict with a personal identity narrative of social responsibility and public health. Or, consider if you were to receive a job offer from a company in an industry with which you grew up (for instance, if your family was in construction, and you received a job offer from a construction company). You would likely understand how the industry works and what constitutes a good job offer, what to expect about the work, and what the work would expect of you. If you received a job offer from within an industry that was new to you, however, you might be at a loss to know what a good salary or benefits constitute, and what the expectations would be on the job.

Research confirms this link between socialization and identity. Russo (1998) studied anticipatory and vocational socialization as factors that lead to the development of occupational/professional identity. In her research with newspaper reporters, journalists talked about how they decided to become reporters early in their lives because they identified with the moral aspect of the job – exposing corruption. In this example, we can see how the socialization into particular careers is heavily influenced by identity commitments.

Various social identities influence our perceptions of similarity or difference with various organizations and related organizational identities. The process of considering a job offer involves negotiating various identities to determine whether the organization is (or could be) something that aligns with who we are (or could be!). One is more likely to accept a job if the organization's identity and the individual's identity have more in common. But even in cases where the fit between an employee's individual identity and organizational identity is disjointed, we can nonetheless see how identity work is engaged to carve out a semi-coherent identity. Research on what is called "dirty work" (Ashforth & Kreiner 1999), for instance, shows how individuals may reframe the work they do as a way to formulate positive individual identities even when they work at organizations deemed taboo – like in garbage collection or in prisons. In a study conducted by Toyoki and Brown (2013), prisoners in a Helsinki prison strategically mitigated their stigmatized identities as prisoners by highlighting their morality and standing as "good people" in order to combat the discourse of prisoners as inherently bad, unworthy or distrustful. Beyond this, Toyoki and Brown connect this kind of identity work to relations of power, in that "prisoners' stigma management strategies were forms of disguise that protected them, verbal challenges to authority that defied the universalizing and homogenizing effects of imprisonment" (p. 18). Socialization, in this way, is not only about aligning with the identities offered by organizations and institutions, but also about distancing oneself from identities that are individually or socially undesirable. This example further demonstrates how even in cases where individuals do not necessarily have the choice to take or reject alignment with an organizational discourse because of "fit" or stigma (perhaps because one needs money to support a family or pay the rent, or because the identity is socially ascribed, as with the case of prisoners), considerable identity work nonetheless takes place.

Other stages of the socialization progression also shape and are shaped by identity processes. The *encounter* stage involves reconciling new organizational experiences in the context of various occupational and personal identities. Attempts at identity regulation are often made by the organization during this early socialization period. The *metamorphosis* stage encompasses negotiating and accepting new roles, which may challenge identity constructs. At the same time, identity constructs may influence the ways in which new organizational roles are enacted, adapted and rejected. The *exit* stage consists of separating from the organization, which not only involves physical separation, but also in cases where one is identified with the organization, identity separation, as one must re-narrate a sense of self. Leaving an organization with which one is highly identified requires extensive identity work. Notably, this identity work does not cease simply because one has exited an organization – can you think of someone who has left a job but continues to talk about the work they used to do or place they used to work (maybe sometimes to an annoying extent)? This happens often, as we apply lessons learned and identity associations from one workplace or situation to a new workplace or situation. Simply leaving the company does not stop us from developing an identity around it, as Bardon, Josserand and Villeseche (2014) demonstrated with members of corporate alumni networks.

Often the research on socialization positions identification as an outcome of organizational socialization practices. As organizations attempt to train employees and get them to buy into the organization's culture through socialization activities, identification is often fostered. Organizational efforts and expenditures on socialization activities like employee orientations, initiation ceremonies and training sessions all potentially influence levels of organizational identification. For instance, research shows that more rigorous socialization programs lead to greater shared values between the organization and the employee (Chatman 1991). Organizational investments in socialization are designed, at least partially, to increase employee identification with the organization. Identification, thus, results as a significant outcome of assimilation processes (Gailliard, Myers & Seibold 2010, p. 571).

All this does not mean, however, that individuals will share the same experiences of the socialization process. Can you think of a time where you and a friend or colleague went through a similar process, but had completely different experiences of it? You might have interpreted the experience differently based on your previous experiences, or even have been treated differently by others within the socialization process. Brenda Allen (1996) used her own experience with this to highlight the "crisis of representation" in organizational communication scholarship that overlooks how race/ethnicity and gender are fundamentally constitutive aspects of organizing (see also Ashcraft & Allen, 2003). In her essay, Allen adopts feminist standpoint theory – a perspective that "advocates using women's everyday lives as a foundation for constructing knowledge and as a basis for criticizing dominant knowledge claims that are based upon men's lives" (p. 258) – to challenge theories of socialization that assume that individuals go through a universal process of socialization and experience it similarly. Yet, in drawing on her own situated experiences of socialization into a US academic institution as a woman of color, Allen highlights the situated and experiential nature of socialization processes. She recalls, for instance, being called on to play specific roles in her department related to minority issues (e.g., to sit on minority interest committees or meet with minority students because she was a woman of color), and messages that she received with patriarchal undertones. Importantly, Allen's experience also demonstrates how race/ethnicity and gender are experienced intersectionally (think back to Chapter 4), as being black as well as a woman compounded to shape her experiences of learning the ropes at her new institution. What is particularly important for the discussion at hand is to recognize the complexity of how identity is at play in organizational constructs. Thus, in all of the topics that we discuss in this chapter (technology, leadership, decision-making, and so forth), we must recognize the situated nature of these constructs. They are not universal constructs, but are experienced differently (or similarly) through intersecting social identities.

Place and Identity

Another area of overlap with organizational and identity scholarship explores how place shapes identity and how identity influences the social construction of places. Often drawing from critical-cultural geography, this research conceives of place as spaces that are imbued with meanings (Gieryn 2000). As symbolic constructions, places represent targets and resources for constructing identities. For example, Larson and Pearson (2012) found that high-tech entrepreneurs in Missoula, Montana utilized discursive resources made available through location such as the opportunity for outdoor recreation. These entrepreneurs saw their careers, at least partly, as ways of enabling a lifestyle and identity related to outdoor recreation like skiing. Certain places, such as a mountain town, provide affordances to construct identities in specific ways.

In addition to places providing resources from which to construct identities, places are also shaped by the social identities of the people located in a particular location. Richard Florida's (2008) research on creative class cities suggests that the congregation of people with certain social identities leads others to want to move into a particular community, thus influencing the meanings associated with that place. For instance, Florida pointed to research that showed that housing values rose as gays and lesbians moved into a neighborhood because the area is thus perceived to be more open and accepting – and all sorts of people prefer to live in such a place. If you've ever said "I'd really like to live there" or "I'd never live there!" your sentiments are, in some way, linked to social identities associated with that place. This shows us how social identities themselves shape the symbolic construction of particular places, demonstrating the utility of a discursive identity lens for understanding related phenomena.

Related to this is how a discursive approach to identity helps to illuminate how identity is embedded in the organizational concept of systems. Akin to Florida's work on creative cities, scholars are increasingly examining "ecosystems" of entrepreneurship and innovation, which are interconnected by shared goals and understandings of work, available resources, and the identity of place and lifestyle. Systems are not merely connected parts, but they are imbued with collective identities that weave throughout, such that the ecosystem itself has an identity. In Waterloo, Canada, for instance, the Waterloo Innovation Ecosystem develops and celebrates their shared identity by hosting an annual high-profile innovation summit, and in the US state of Utah, members of the innovation ecosystem have identified themselves as the "Silicon

Slopes" as a way to identify nationally (with Silicon Valley) and also locally (with the ski slopes of the nearby mountain ranges). What we think is forward-thinking about examining the identity of innovation ecosystems is that it begins to help us better theorize what has been referred to as a "collective-associative" identity, or the identity of a collective that is generated by the very people who associate with that collective (we discussed this in terms of Ashcraft's (2013) glass slipper metaphor in previous chapters). One example of this is research into entrepreneur networks, which promise access to resources for members but also develop a collective identity from the members who associate with the network (Gill & Barbour 2016). This research shows how, although we often think of entrepreneurs as acting alone, they not only act collectively but develop collective identities. This kind of understanding could be applied to a number of workers and employees who are often considered to work alone, but in actuality, work within an interconnected, holistic system. Thus, the application of identity work and regulation to collectives (rather than individuals) is a means to understand the systemic nature of identity in an ever-connected world.

Concluding Thoughts

Identity research informs and is informed by other areas of organizational research. It is likely that future advancements in the identity research will link identity with other concepts, especially as these other concepts are understood from different interdisciplinary perspectives. Studying identity (or anything else in social science for that matter) as disconnected from other social processes doesn't make much sense in an interdisciplinary and interconnected understanding of the world.

Discussion Questions

1. In what ways does your own use of technologies shape your identity? How do you use social media to communicate your identity? Which social media send what messages about your social identity? For example, if you Snapchat someone what does that say about you and your relationship with that person?

2. How much of social identity in contemporary college life is negotiated on social media? What are the advantages of this? Disadvantages? How difficult would identity work be for you with your current group of friends without social media?

3. Think about your experience of leadership in your life. Specifically, can you think of a time that you were positioned as a leader but did not feel like one, or a time when you did not have a leadership position but still felt like a leader? What influenced how you felt, and why?

4. Brenda Allen's experience of new faculty member socialization highlights how the assumptions people make about our social identities influences our work experiences, as well as how these assumptions interact with other organizational constructs. When have you been in a situation where assumptions about your social identity were used as justification for decisions made about your work preferences and skills?

5. What does the place in which you live say about your identity? What identity narratives are made available/unavailable by the place in which you live? When you tell someone where you are from, how much does that reflect your identity? In what ways do you communicate to associate yourself or disassociate yourself with a place to frame who you are to others?

7

Researching and Practicing Identity

More and more, researchers and practitioners are recognizing that identity, place and culture are central to the development of a region. We see this particularly with regional development around innovation, a hot topic in today's entrepreneurial and innovation age. Consider the case of Aaliyah, who is on the economic development team for a mid-sized metropolitan city with a population size of 1 million, an increasingly diverse migrant community and a strong history and culture of individualism. Aaliyah's education and training is in the social sciences, so she has been tasked with understanding the interests and identity of the people who live in the region, and providing input into the economic development plan based on this. Specifically, Aaliyah will need to consider what influences people in the region to choose the work they do and how they make sense of it, what they hope to see for development in their city and whether or not proposed developments will be successful based on the shared regional identity. Given the complexity of identity that we have described in this book, what are the methods she might consider adopting for a study like this? How might Aaliyah begin to "see" identity in this metropolitan area? In this chapter, we provide insight into what choices Aaliyah might make for gathering and presenting data by discussing the meta-theoretical implications of a discursive approach to identity, the methods that researchers commonly adopt when studying identity and the implications for practice from a discursive identity approach.

Methodological Commitments in the Discursive Study of Identity

As a way of beginning, we first want to revisit our discussion of meta-theory from Chapter 2 as a way to clarify how the commitments that accompany discursive identity research may inform the choices scholars make regarding methods. Because a discursive approach to identity embraces a view on identity as socially constructed, research in this vein tends to be grounded in interpretive meta-theoretical commitments. An interpretive ontology posits reality as socially constructed and as such, assumes that multiple realities, based in individuals' perceptions and understandings, exist simultaneously (Cheney 2000). Interpretive ontologies generally do not place any particular "frame" or bounded construct around these realities, and as such, it is generally thought that individuals are fairly free in their realities, capable of improvisational action and "making things up" as they go. Epistemologically, interpretivism assumes that knowledge is a product of one's subjective and also intersubjectively negotiated position in society, created through interactions and the shared use of language and symbols. In interpretive approaches, knowledge is a localized phenomenon constructed within particular contexts and situations (Cheney 2000). Accordingly, methods that recognize and explore the possibility of multiple, and shifting, understandings of self are often adopted in identity research.

Many researchers also adopt a critical lens when studying identity from a discursive approach, even if only indirectly, because of an inherent recognition of the centrality of power and subjectivity in discourse. A discursive approach to identity that is grounded in Foucault, but also influenced by other Critical theorists such as Butler, Marx, the Frankfurt School and others, shifts the focus away from the description of open and multiple lived experiences and realities to also interrogate how society and individuals are bounded in broad power dimensions that operate as central organizing features of reality, particularly of the public sphere (Mumby 2000). Critical theorists believe that dominant and, often, dominating ideologies are the mechanism by which totalizing systems of oppression are created, and where discursive power relations maintain distinctions between advantaged and disadvantaged classes.

Scholars in organization studies have also adopted feminist discursive approaches to identity research, focusing on dimensions of difference and the construction of occupational legitimacy in identity construction. As we discussed in Chapter 4, although feminist approaches have a history of prioritizing gender over other social identities, or even studying gender in isolation, attention to intersectionality and the ways that social identities intersect to compound privilege and disadvantage have been gaining traction. A poststructural feminist lens, in particular, is well-aligned with a discursive approach to identity because it challenges the pre-existence of identity categories and instead looks to uncover how labels and categories are themselves socially constructed (Butler 1995; McDonald 2015). Through this lens, we are able to examine how identity markers come to be considered "normal" versus "abnormal" and therefore how people construct a sense of self through occupational and social identity discourses that are delicate, tentative and shifting.

Researching the Discursive Construction of Identity

Scholars who study identity from a discursive approach tend to adopt qualitative approaches to data collection that include interviewing and participant observation. This is not to say that quantitative methods cannot be engaged, but that interpretive commitments that encourage researchers to dialogue with participants are often more easily facilitated through qualitative methods. As we discuss below, scholars who research identity from discursive approaches strive to construct an understanding that is rich and in-depth. Rather than review the foundational practices that are involved in undertaking certain qualitative methods (see Lindlof & Taylor 2011; Tracy 2013), we instead focus on the rationale for adopting (and combining) particular methods to illuminate the range and variety of techniques in use by discursive identity scholars.

Historical and Textual Analysis

One of the increasing hallmarks of identity research from a discursive approach is that it places identity within a larger discursive, and material, context. Ashcraft (2005; 2007; Ashcraft & Mumby 2004), in particular, has argued for the historical consideration of identity as formed in conjunction with entrenched and enduring discourses of occupation. In her analysis of the occupational identities of commercial flight attendants and airline pilots, Ashcraft demonstrates how the role of "pilot" and "flight attendant" were created at the intersection of an emerging industry, media coverage and expectations for gender and ethnicity vis-à-vis work. To do this, Ashcraft traced the development of these occupations through early corporate and industry texts, as well as the media coverage of the pilots and their feats that captured imaginations in the early days of this industry. By uncovering the historical origins of these occupations, Ashcraft is able to better illuminate how and why people working in these occupations *today* grapple with and perform the occupational identity work that they do.

Relatedly, scholars often engage in textual analysis of relevant macro- or meso-level materials to paint a picture of a more localized context, for instance national cultural attitudes toward gender, ethnicity and work (e.g., Essers & Benschop 2007; 2008); expectations for and framing of work in mainstream business publications (Gill 2013; 2014; Holmer Nadesan 2001; Holmer Nadesan & Trethewey 2000; Trethewey 2001); or the policies and attitude of a particular organization (Holmer Nadesan 1996; Sveningsson & Alvesson 2003). Textual analysis along these lines provides an understanding of the discourse in circulation, and often serves as the foundational context of identity research. Alvesson and Wilmott (2002) argue that this is the case, for instance, with identity regulation, where "induction, training and promotion procedures are developed in ways that have implications for the shaping and direction of identity" (p. 625). Indeed, communication and discourse scholarship has a rich history of textual and rhetorical examination of how organizational artifacts shape the ideal identity within an organization.

Case Studies

Studying identity may also take the form of a case study, which focuses on one or a small group of individuals and explores their identity construction in-depth. Sveningsson and Alvesson (2003), for instance, present the case of "H" as a way to understand her own identity construction in the context of the organization in which she works, reasoning that "the level of senior middle manager may then be a way of making significant parts of organizations visible – actors then are seen as sites or entrances for less visible organizational conditions and processes" (p. 1169). To accomplish this, the authors conducted several interviews with H and dozens of interviews with managers and employees around her, and also attended and observed management meetings over approximately 14 months. In these efforts, their focus was on the "roles, expectations, coordinating efforts of the heroine, globalization and the managing of knowledge-intensive companies in general" (p. 1170) so as to generate a sense of the discourses in circulation at the company, and the ways that H navigated them in constructing an identity narrative for herself.

Case studies or extended biographies offer an important means to study the complexity of identity construction and identity work. Down and Reveley's (2009) case study of Wilson the Utilities Technician, a front-line supervisor at a coal plant, involved a year-long study of Wilson that took place as part of a longer six-year study. During this time, the researchers were able to observe Wilson navigate his ascension to *de facto* supervisor, and his hesitancy at taking on this role, through a combination of interviews and observation. Observation was crucial in understanding Wilson's experience, because it allowed the researchers to "capture contextual features of spoken interaction that cannot be easily obtained through tape-recording alone" (p. 386), and therefore helped to enrich the individual account of identity work that was encapsulated in interviews. That is, the study "sought to avoid the pitfalls of generating a theoretically self-fulfilling view of identity work as a purely self-narrational or discursive process" (pp. 386–387).

Participant Observation and Ethnographically Spirited Methods

Participant observation, usually combined with interviews, is commonly adopted by identity scholars as a way to examine the invisibility of identity work and the practices that are involved in it. Not only can participant observation (or a version thereof) provide a sense of identity construction from the participants' point of view, but it helps to demonstrate the everyday, active and/ or passive (Wieland 2010) ways that people construct an identity. Tracy (2000), for instance, notes that her participant observation on the Radiant Spirit cruise ship gave her "access to inside motivations and behaviors that cruise staff are well trained to regularly hide from the public" (p. 101). Building on this kind of rationale, we see shadowing emerging as a fitting kind of participant observation, not only because shadowing provides insider access but also due to the recognition that post or late modern "organizing happens in many places at once, and organizers move around quickly and frequently" (Czarniawska 2007, p. 16; Gill 2011). Participant observation and shadowing are therefore often utilized to study habitus (Alvesson 1994) or the *accomplishment* of identity. For instance, Bruni's (Bruni, Gherardi & Poggio 2004) insider access to the everyday negotiation of identity meant that he was able to understand how concepts such as gender and entrepreneurship were accomplished in interaction, or performed, with others. Moreover, research in this vein addresses the interaction of spatial layout at work as it supports and/or challenges occupational identity (Dean, Gill & Barbour 2016; Halford & Leonard 2006).

Expanding on this, identity research has more recently embraced a combination of methods. We refer to this as "ethnographically spirited" because although such methods do not necessarily reproduce the kinds of traditional ethnographies that are carried out for years in one field, they do approximate the rich, detailed, intense and complex layering of data that comes from in-depth study (Tracy 2013; Van Maanen 2006). Musson and Duberly (2007) for instance, adopted a combination of in-depth interviews and observation methods, which allowed them to tack between an understanding of the organizational context and the identity construction of the employees within the organization. Wells, Gill and McDonald's (2015) study of the identity construction of highly skilled, foreign-born scientists in the US combines interviews and observations of three participants with the first author's entrenched history of working within that particular organization. And, Wieland's (2010) examination of "ideal selves" combined "observing, asking, and collecting" to present a rounded understanding of the research site.

In these kinds of studies, surveys and quantitative measures are sometimes used to identify attitudes, tensions or disjunctures that then inform or supplement qualitative interviews. Wells (2013), for instance, surveyed 141 analytic chemists about the tasks that comprised their work and their attitudes toward diversity in their field, conducting in-depth interviews with twenty-two respondents. Identifying a disjuncture between the quantitative responses and qualitative answers of US-born scientists led Wells to interrogate the role that language and national identity play in constructions of a "good analytical chemist." Holmer Nadesan (1996) provides a further example of a deep layering of methods, gathering data through five distinct, but related, methods. In studying the hierarchy and identity work of service employees in a university residential graduate house, Holmer Nadesan undertook textual analysis of relevant job materials; distributed an open-ended survey amongst participants that encouraged them to discuss their work and identity in their own ways; interviewed the house staff and students who lived there to gain a nuanced understanding of what the job "actually" entails as well as the perceptions of it; observed the house staff to gain a richer sense of daily habits and routines; and finally, attended University HR-type sessions to understand how service work was positioned within the broader University attention to HR.

Interviews and Discursive Resources

Responding to the persuasive critique that interviews are inef-
fective for capturing identity construction because they are only
able to represent a participant's *perception* of their work and
identity (see, e.g., Alvesson 2003), discursive identity research
saw a shift away from interview-only studies of identity. More
recently, however, scholars are returning to the interview as a core
element in identity research. Scholars advocate that interviews
provide a way to understand how people *account* for their identity
(e.g., Kuhn 2006; 2009; Larson & Tompkins 2005; Tompkins
& Cheney 1983) by mobilizing certain interpretive repertoires
(Wetherell et al. 2001) or discursive resources, where discursive
resources refer to key metaphors, images, words, phrases and so
forth that represent particular discourses in identity construction.
In a study examining how lawyers responded to accusations of
being "corporate lackeys," Kuhn (2009) explains that the "task
was to understand the discursive resources offered in response" to
the accusation, and that:

> My expectation ... was that respondents would appropriate cultural
> scripts and provide evidence of the discourses comprising their subject
> position. Explaining their position to an outsider, the respondents'
> inexperience and their precarious employment status together suggest
> that responses were not straightforward expressions of interiorities,
> but were instead the result of tentative and contingent identifications
> with those multiple discourses. This was precisely the aim. (p. 688)

Further to this point, in our own work regarding entrepreneurial
identity (Gill & Larson 2014), we also embraced interviews as
ways to capture the discursive resources utilized in the construction of identity for self-identified entrepreneurs *because* we wanted
to understand how they made sense of their work first and fore-
most, and the degree to which they drew on discourses at the
macro/national and regional/meso levels. As we argued, because
entrepreneurs do not always have a formal, distinct "organization" to provide organizational context, they rely on macro- and

meso-level discourses of entrepreneurship and organization that circulate outside of the traditional organizational walls (see also Tracy & Trethewey 2005).

The use of interviews to uncover identity and the related critiques of this method (Alvesson 2003) for that very purpose illustrate the importance of aligning methods with meta-theoretical commitments. If interviews are framed by researchers as a means to gain insight into a "true" inner identity then, indeed, interviews are likely insufficient to understand identity. On the other hand, if interviews are framed as verbal sense-making opportunities (Larson & Pepper 2003) that reveal the discursive resources (Kuhn 2006) that participants use to strategically narrate their identities in the context of the interview conversation, then interviews are a useful methodological resource. From an interpretive perspective, verbal sense-making occurs in a variety of contexts and interviews are one such context in which identities are articulated. Put differently, interview discourse is discourse-in-context that is no less "real" than discourse in other contexts. The key for researchers is to be conscious and explicit about the types of claims that different types of discursive data allow the researcher to make.

Biographical or Life Narratives

For similar reasons, biographical, or life, narratives have become an accepted way of studying identity from a discursive perspective, possibly because of the depth that can be achieved in such interviews. A method incorporated into the sociology discipline since at least the 1930s (Watson 2009), biographical or life narratives (also referred to as life histories) involve in-depth interviews that sometimes span hours or even take place over a series of meetings that encourage participants to recall and explore meaningful events, turning points and experiences in their lives, essentially sense-making their experiences in conjunction with the researcher. Despite some debate about the centrality of narrative and stories to the lives of individuals, life histories continue to represent a popular and powerful method for capturing identity, and as Watson (2009) reminds us, *"human beings are cultural animals.*

Narratives and stories play their part in the lives of all of us, *regardless of whether we are particularly self-conscious about it"* (p. 429, emphasis in original). For his part, Watson argues that this provides justification for studying published autobiographies as "relatively highly crafted presentation[s] of self which, in turn, enables us to examine some of the finer nuances of identity work" (p. 432). Beyond this, many scholars undertake life narrative methods in real-time interviews. Essers and Benschop (2007), for instance, asked participants to recall their life stories as "chapters" around the salient moments in their lives.

Photovoice

An emerging method in organization studies, photovoice, or photoelicitation, is informed by anthropological approaches to the lifeworld. This method asks participants to visually represent some aspect of their lives, often by using disposable cameras or cameras on smart phones (Wang 1999), bolstered by the argument that "methodologies relying solely on spoken or written texts may be inadequate to understand the performative character of human relationships with the objects and spaces they move through (and that move through them)" (Shortt & Warren 2012, p. 18). Once the images are printed or otherwise available, the researcher discusses them one-on-one or in a focus group with participants with the goal of surfacing the key ideas represented in the images. Thus, espoused benefits of photovoice are that it assists participants in highlighting parts of their experience that may be otherwise invisible or inaccessible (Slutskaya, Simpson & Hughes 2012), and encourages participants in co-constructing research findings because they are able to initially determine what is meaningful to them, and then partake in a sense-making discussion around it (Novak 2010; Wang & Burris 1994).

One work-based example of this can be found in Shortt's studies of the "identityscapes" of hairdressers (Shortt 2012; Shortt & Warren 2012). Noting that "as well as representing the narration of identity through the medium of material objects and space (e.g., visual narratives in and of themselves – akin to a photo essay), the photographs generated textual and inter-textual narratives of words during the interviews" (p. 23), Shortt and Warren (2012) identified four different ways that photographs help to illuminate the work identity of their participants. Specifically, *self-portraits* provide insight into how a participant wants to narrate a sense of self; photos of *odd or unusual spaces* at work demonstrate behind-the-scenes dimensions of a work identity; *everyday objects* and qualities of space (e.g., scuffs on the floor surrounding a hair-cutting chair) showcase the mundane and familiar as evocative of one's identity; and *"silly"* photographs demonstrate creative identity and deviation from the norm. Findings from Shortt's research reflect some of what Slutskaya, Simpson and Hughes (2012) evidenced in their photovoice study of male butchers, where participants were able to express appreciation for the aesthetic dimensions of their trade that would likely not have surfaced (as fully) in interviews, as well as expressions of nostalgia for fading skill sets and fragmenting communities.

Reflexivity

Because of the inherent recognition of relations of power in discursive approaches to identity, identity scholars tend to conduct research with an eye toward also adopting reflexive techniques. There are a number of ways to define reflexivity (as we did so previously in regards to reflexivity in identity work), and practices linked to them, but for our purposes in this chapter we want to define reflexivity methodologically as the recognition of the role that a researcher herself or himself plays in data collection and analysis. A commitment to embracing reflexivity means that a researcher strives to recognize how their own participation shapes the data available to be collected, even in topic selection. Identity scholars who seek to be reflexive often emphasize the co-constructed nature of their research, looking for opportunities to highlight participant voices. Essers and Benshop (2007), for instance, underscore that the life narrative interviews they conducted were not just stories told by participants, but were "linguistic constructions made in close interaction with the

166

researcher" (p. 56). As such, discursive identity researchers must manage they ways in which their own identities might shape the discursive expression of identity from others.

Practicing a Discursive Approach to Organizations and Identity

In this final section of the book, we aim to stress the practical benefits of understanding identity from a discursive perspective. In previous chapters, we discussed contemporary factors that make identity especially relevant for modern scholarship and many of these same factors make identity particularly critical for organizational practitioners. This is because:

> Ironically, as societies and organizations become more turbulent and individual–organization relationships become more tenuous, individuals' desire for some kind of work-based identification is likely to increase – precisely because traditional moorings are increasingly unreliable. (Ashforth et al. 2008, p. 326)

Put another way, individuals look to workplace organizations and other organizations to provide many of the discursive resources that they use to narrate their identities. As a result, it is critical for both employees and employers to pay attention to identity.

For employees (organization members) several identity-related practical concerns come to the fore. First, organization members should be aware of the ways in which organizations may attempt to shape their identities. Control is necessary in organizations and there are even appealing aspects to identity control (i.e., being part of something larger than yourself), but this type of control must also be deconstructed and assessed by individuals. Organizational identity control is often subtle and unobtrusive, yet powerful, so bringing this out into the open and into conversation with other potential identity possibilities makes sense for employees. For instance, it is okay to identify strongly with work, but one should also take stock as to why one is so strongly identified with a particular organization and to evaluate the consequences for an overall identity and relationships.

Second, it is important to be aware of one's own identity management practices. The ways in which we manage multiple identities impacts our health and happiness. For instance, Tracy and Trethewey (2005) point to the negative emotional consequences for employees who pressure themselves into finding an elusive "real self." The popular metaphor of a "real self" or a "true self" sometimes leads to frustrations in a world where most individuals take on numerous identities in different contexts. These scholars offer the alternative metaphor of a "crystalized identity" as a more empowering way to get out of the true self trap of trying to talk about the different aspects of one's identity. Such a metaphor might, for example, relieve some guilt employees feel when they have to act one way at work and a very different way at home.

For employers, a discursive approach to studying organizations and identities suggests that owners/managers need to pay attention to identity as an important variable that underlies many different organizational processes. With all the attention paid to human resources, recruitment and socialization, an identity lens helps to explain how employees act according to the ways in which they construct their identities. Discourse from managers, whether intentional or not, contains resources that employees can use to manage their identities. Talk matters greatly in the process of constructing identities as discourse/Discourse provides the building blocks for identity – the discursive resources that we all use to narrate our identities. In such an environment, consciously framing messages with identity concerns in mind makes sense for managers. Managers should be conscious of the ways in which the narratives celebrated and sanctioned by the organization are used to shape and control employees' identities.

The ability of employing organizations to shape and control employee identities surfaces important ethical considerations for employers and employees. Identity control is a powerful resource for organizations, but also creates opportunities for abuse. Employers must understand their inherent power to shape identities and do so in responsible ways. From our perspective, ethical identity control involves openness to and respect for other (external) possible discourses of identity, encouragement to bring other perspectives into the conversation, candidness as to organizational efforts to shape identities and encouragement of more holistic identities that take into account other (personal) aspects of life. Our contention is not that identity control is inherently unethical, and we acknowledge that it is likely inevitable in contemporary society. On the other hand, the choices that employers make and the ways that they go about implementing normative types of control can be accomplished in more (or less) ethical ways.

A discursive approach to managing identities might also offer practical assistance to communities attempting to attract workers to particular regions. Our own previously discussed research on high-tech entrepreneurial identities offers prescriptions for community leaders as to how to market particular regions to prospective workers. For example, in Missoula, Montana, an entrepreneurial identity that combines high-tech work with work-life balance and an outdoor recreation ethic appeals to the entrepreneurs drawn to this region. Marketing efforts from community leaders should therefore celebrate and extoll the unique high-tech identity of the region, rather then trying to become another Silicon Valley. For many residents of Silicon Valley, this discourse would not be appealing, but for others, perhaps as they sit on grid-locked freeways on their way to work, such an alternative work/life identity might have great appeal.

We conclude this section with what we see as an instructive long-term example of using discursive identity principles to foster organizational and social change. Organizational communication scholar Phil Tompkins began volunteer work at the St. Francis Center, a homeless shelter, in Denver, Colorado after retiring from the University of Colorado in 1998. When he started at the St. Francis Center he didn't know much about homelessness or the organization – he just responded to a request for help one week. Over the course of many years of volunteering at the St. Francis Center, Phil became identified with both the center and the "guests" of the shelter. As a result of this strong sense of identification,

Phil began to learn more about homelessness and ultimately became an advocate for ending homelessness in Denver. In his book-length treatment of his experiences, *Who Is My Neighbor?: Communicating and Organizing to End Homelessness* (2009), Tompkins details his journey into learning more about homelessness and taking a leadership role in a social movement to end homelessness in his community. He also explicitly acknowledges how his own identity was shaped by his identifications – in his own words, he became an "abolitionist" for the cause of homelessness.

In addition to personally narrating an identity as an abolitionist, Tompkins also drew on his own years of studying organizational identification, from a rhetorical and discursive perspective, in his quest to understand homelessness and participate in solutions. For instance, he began to think of homelessness as a form of "alienation" from organizations or the lack of connection to organizations and society. Tompkins wrote:

> Homeless people are alienated from society and organizations because they no longer find them *reasonable*. Nor do we domiciled people identify with them. This rejection serves as an additional stigma. As Mother Teresa said of her work among the poorest of the poor in Calcutta, 'We know that being unwanted is the greatest disease of all.' (pp. 59–60, emphasis in original)

The discourses available for identity construction by the homeless are thus shaped by the ways that others see and interact with the homeless. In addition to helping to understanding homelessness, Tompkins also uses the identity lens to try to explain how very different groups (e.g., homeless advocates, neighborhood association, business owners, government officials) came together to agree on a plan to end homelessness in Denver. Although these groups were very different on the surface (i.e., not highly identified), they respectfully listened to each other through numerous group meetings and realized that they shared the common goal of reducing the homeless population on Denver's streets. They were able to achieve consensus through a give-and-take, communicative process that constructed a shared sense of purpose for solving the homeless problem in Denver.

In this extended example, we see identification and identity appearing in ways that are consequential for organizational practice. First, we see how motivation for organizational and social change comes from our identifications and identities. Phil didn't start out to become an abolitionist to end homelessness in his community, but he began to narrate his own identity in ways where he identified with the St. Francis Center and the homeless guests of the center. Second, we see how a discursive perspective on organizations and identity can shape an understanding of organizational problems and the solutions to those problems. Viewing identity construction, including identification, as basic human needs leads one to consider the consequences of social alienation. In addition, the discursive construction of some sort of common ground was necessary amongst the many different participants that came together to formulate a plan to enact social change.

Concluding Thoughts

At first glance, researching identity seems like a difficult, if not impossible, task. As we have indicated throughout this book, identity is an abstract, complex and fluid phenomenon that can be difficult to ascertain. And yet, although researching identity poses particular challenges, it also offers exciting and intriguing opportunities to learn about others. Nonetheless, there are important considerations and choices in identity research that we touched on in this chapter. It is our contention that a discursive identity lens offers researchers an avenue to uncover necessary understandings about a fundamental factor and process of organizational life and to link identity to other important organizational constructs. In addition, we see an identity lens as a critical consideration for organizational practitioners as identity remains a major challenge for most in the modern world.

Discussion Questions

1. What methods do you think are best for studying identity? What are interviews likely to reveal about identity? What are interviews not likely to reveal about identity?
2. How would you engage in reflexive practice in your own identity research? How might being reflexive shape what you notice (or miss) about the data you are collecting?
3. Think of the place where you grew up or a place to which you feel very attached. What are the identity discourses associated with this place or region? Are there particular occupations and assumptions about work that are entwined with this place?
4. At the practical level, what have you learned from this book about identity that might influence how you reflect on and manage your own identity? What might you have learned that would help you advise others who are struggling with identity issues?
5. What are the practical advantages of a discursive understanding of identity? What productive ways does this approach help you think and act in regards to identity?

References

Aakhus, M., Ballard, D., Flanagin, A., Kuhn, T., Leonardi, P., Mease, J. & Miller, K. (2011) Communication and materiality: A conversation from the CM Café. *Communication Monographs* 78, 557–568.

Acker, J. (1990) Hierarchies, jobs, bodies: A theory of gendered organizations. *Gender & Society* 4, 139–158.

Acker, J. (2012) Gendered organizations and intersectionality: Problems and possibilities. *Equality, Diversity and Inclusion: An International Journal* 31, 214–224.

Adib, A. & Guerrier, Y. (2003) The interlocking of gender with nationality, race, ethnicity and class: The narratives of women in hotel work. *Gender, Work and Organization* 10, 413–432.

Ainsworth, S. & Hardy, C. (2004) Discourse and identities. In Grant, D., Hardy, C., Oswick, C. & Putnam, L. (eds.). *The Sage Handbook of Organizational Discourse*. Sage Publication, London, pp. 153–174.

Albert, S. & Whetten, D. A. (1985) Organizational identity. *Research in Organizational Behavior* 7, 263–295.

Alboher, M. (2007) When it comes to careers, change is a constant. *The New York Times* [online], 1 May 2007. Available from: http://nyti.ms/1RKuEdm.

Allen, B. J. (1996) Feminist standpoint theory: A black woman's (re)view of organizational socialization. *Communication Studies* 47, 257–271.

Allen, B. J. (2011) *Difference Matters: Communicating Social Identity*, 2nd edn. Waveland Press, Prospect Heights, IL.

Alvesson, M. (1994) Talking in organizations: Managing identity and impressions in an advertising agency. *Organization Studies* 15, 535–563.

Alvesson, M. (2003) Beyond neo-positivism, romanticism and localism: A reflexive approach to interviews. *Academy of Management Review* 28, 13–33.

Alvesson, M. (2010) Self-doubters, strugglers, storytellers, surfers and others: Images of self-identities in organization studies. *Human Relations* 63, 193–217.

Alvesson, M., Ashcraft, K. L. & Thomas, R. (2008) Identity matters: Reflections on the construction of identity scholarship in organization studies. *Organization* 15, 5–28.

Alvesson, M. & Karreman, D. (2000) Varieties of discourse: On the study of organizations through discourse analysis. *Human Relations* 53, 1125–1149.

Alvesson, M. and Willmott, H. (2002) Identity regulation as organizational control: Producing the appropriate individual. *Journal of Management Studies* 39, 619–644.

Aristotle (1954) Rhetoric. Trans. Rhys Roberts, W. In McKeon, R. (ed.) *The Basic Works of Aristotle*. Random House, New York.

Ashcraft, K. L. (2005) Resistance through consent? Occupational identity, organizational form, and the maintenance of masculinity among commercial airline pilots. *Management Communication Quarterly* 19, 67–90.

Ashcraft, K. L. (2007) Appreciating the "work" of discourse: Occupational identity and difference as organizing mechanisms in the case of commercial airline pilots. *Discourse & Communication* 1, 9–36.

Ashcraft, K. L. (2011) Knowing "work" through the communication of difference: A revised agenda for difference studies. In Mumby, D. K. (ed.) *Reframing Difference in Organizational Communication Studies: Research, Pedagogy, and Practice*. Sage Publications, Thousand Oaks, CA, pp. 3–30.

Ashcraft, K. L. (2013) The glass slipper: "Incorporating" occupational identity in management studies. *Academy of Management Review* 38, 6–31.

Ashcraft, K. L. & Allen, B. J. (2003) The racial foundation of organizational communication. *Communication Theory* 13, 5–38.

Ashcraft, K. L. & Mumby, D. K. (2004) *Reworking Gender: A Feminist Communicology of Organization*. Sage Publications, Thousand Oaks, CA.

Ashforth, B. E. & Kreiner, G. E. (1999) "How can you do it?": Dirty work and the challenge of constructing a positive identity. *Academy of Management Review* 24, 413–434.

Ashforth, B. E. & Mael, F. (1989) Social identity theory and the organization. *Academy of Management Review* 14, 20–39.

Ashforth, B. E. and Mael, F. (1996) Organizational identity and strategy as a context for the individual. In Baum, J. A. C. & Dutton, J. E. (eds.) *Advances in strategic management*, JIA, Greenwich, CT, vol. 13, pp. 17–62.

Ashforth, B. E., Harrison, S. H. & Corley, K. G. (2008) Identification in organizations: An examination of four fundamental questions. *Journal of Management*, 34, 325–374.

Attkisson, S. (2010) Following the aid money to Haiti. *CBS News* [online], 12 July 2010. Available from: http://www.cbsnews.com/8301–18563_162–6477611.html.

Avolio, B. J. & Gardner, W. L. (2005) Authentic leadership development: Getting to the root of positive forms of leadership. *The Leadership Quarterly* 16, 315–338.

References

Bardon, T., Josserand, E. & Villeseche, F. (2014) Beyond nostalgia: Identity work in corporate alumni networks. *Human Relations* 68, 1–24.

Barker, J. R. (1993) Tightening the iron cage: Concertive control in self-managing teams. *Administrative Science Quarterly* 38, 408–437.

Barker, J. R. (1999) *The Discipline of Teamwork: Participation and Concertive Control.* Sage Publications, Thousand Oaks, CA.

Barker, J. R. & Tompkins, P. K. (1994) Identification in the self-managing organization: Characteristics of target and tenure. *Human Communication Research* 21, 223–240.

Barley, S. R. & Kunda, G. (1992) Design and devotion: Surges of rational and normative ideologies of control in managerial discourse. *Administrative Science Quarterly* 37, 363–399.

Barley, S. R. & Kunda, G. (2001) Bringing work back in. *Organization Science* 12, 76–95.

Barnard, C. I. (1938) *The Functions of the Executive.* Harvard University Press, Cambridge, MA.

Berger, P. L. & Luckmann, T. (1967) *The Social Construction of Reality: A Treatise in the Sociology of Knowledge.* The Penguin Press, New York.

Best, S. & Kellner, D. (1991) *Postmodern Theory: Critical Interrogations.* Guilford Press, New York.

Bialik, C. (2010) Seven careers in a lifetime? Think twice, research says. *The Wall Street Journal* [online], 4 September 2010. Available from: http://www.wsj.com/articles/SB10001424052748704206804575468162805877990.

Boje, D. M. (1995) Stories of the storytelling organization: A postmodern analysis of Disney as "Tamara-Land." *Academy of Management Journal* 38, 997–1035.

Boogaard, B. & Roggeband, C. (2010) Paradoxes of intersectionality: Theorizing inequality in the Dutch police force through structure and agency. *Organization* 17, 53–75.

Borger, J. (2016) Refugee arrivals in Greece exceed 100,000 in less than two months. *Guardian* [online], 23 February 2016. Available from: http://www.theguardian.com/world/2016/feb/23/number-of-refugee-arrivals-in-greece-passes-100000–in-less-than-two-months.

Bowman, K. (2009) A killer tax. *Forbes* [online], 7 December 2009. Available from: http://www.forbes.com/2009/12/04/polls-estate-death-tax-opinions-columnists-karlyn-bowman.html.

Braverman, H. (1976) *Labour and Monopoly Capital: The Degradation of Work in the Twentieth Century.* Monthly Review Press, New York.

Brummans, B. H. J. M., Cooren, F., Robichaud, D. and Taylor, J. R., 2014. Approaches to the communicative constitution of organizations. *The SAGE Handbook of Organizational Communication: Advances in Theory, Research, and Methods*, pp. 173–194.

Bruni A., Gherardi, S. & Poggio, B. (2004) Doing gender, doing entrepreneurship:

An ethnographic account of intertwined practices. *Gender, Work & Organization* 11, 406–429.

Bryman, A. (1996) Leadership in organizations. In Clegg, S. R., Hardy, C. & Nord, W. R. (eds.) *Handbook of Organization Studies*. Sage Publications, London, pp. 276–292.

Bullis, C. & Bach, B. W. (1989a) Are mentor relationships helping organizations? An exploration of developing mentee-mentor-organizational identifications using turning point analysis. *Communication Quarterly* 37, 119–213.

Bullis, C. & Bach, B. W. (1989b) Socialization turning points: An examination of change in organizational identification. *Western Journal of Speech Communication* 53, 273–293.

Bullis, C. & Bach, B. W. (1991) An explication and test of communication network content and multiplexity as predictors of organizational identification. *Western Journal of Speech Communication* 55, 180–197.

Bullis, C. & Tompkins, P. K. (1989) The forest ranger revisited: A study of control practices and identification. *Communication Monographs* 56, 287–306.

Burke, K. (1973) The rhetorical situation. In Thayer, L. (ed.) *Communication: Ethical and Moral Issues*. Gordon and Breach, London, pp. 263–275.

Burke, K. (1984) *Attitudes Toward History*. University of California Press, Berkeley, CA.

Burrell, G. & Morgan, G. (1979) *Sociological Paradigms and Organisational Analysis*. Heinemann, London.

Butler, J. (1995) Contingent foundations: Feminism and the question of postmodernism. In Benhabib, S., Butler, J., Cornell, D. & Fraser, N. (eds.) *Feminist Contentions: A Philosophical Exchange*. Routledge, New York, pp. 35–57.

Buzzanell, P. M. (1994) Gaining a voice: Feminist organizational communication theorizing. *Management Communication Quarterly* 7, 339–383.

Calás, M. B. & Smircich, L. (1991) Voicing seduction to silence leadership. *Organization Studies* 12, 567–601.

Calmes, J. (2016) Harriet Tubman ousts Andrew Jackson in change for a $20. *The New York Times* [online], 20 April 2016. Available from: http://www.nytimes.com/2016/04/21/us/women-currency-treasury-harriet-tubman.html?_r=0.

Carlone, D. & Taylor, B. (1998) Organizational communication and cultural studies: A review essay. *Communication Theory* 8, 337–367.

Carroll, B. & Levy, L. (2010) Leadership development as identity construction. *Management Communication Quarterly* 24, 211–231.

Chatman, J. A. (1991) Matching people and organizations: Selection and socialization in public accounting firms. *Administrative Science Quarterly* 36, 459–484.

Cheney, G. (1982) Identification as process and product: a field study. Unpublished master's thesis, Purdue University.

References

Cheney, G. (1983) On the various and changing meanings of organizational membership: A field study of organizational identification. *Communication Monographs* 50, 342–362.

Cheney, G. (1991) *Rhetoric in an Organizational Society: Managing Multiple Identities*. University of South Carolina Press, Columbia.

Cheney, G. (2000) Interpreting interpretive research: Towards perspectivism without relativism. In Corman, S. R. & Poole, M. S. (eds.) *Perspectives on Organizational Communication: Finding Common Ground*. The Guilford Press, New York, pp. 17–45.

Cheney, G. (2005) Theorizing about rhetoric and organizations: Classical, interpretive and critical aspects. In May, S. & Mumby, D. K. (eds.) *Engaging Organizational Communication Theory and Research: Multiple Perspectives*. Sage Publications, Thousand Oaks, CA, pp. 55–84.

Cheney, G. & Ashcraft, K. L. (2007) Considering "the professional" in communication studies: Implications for theory and research within and beyond the boundaries of organizational communication. *Communication Theory* 17, 146–175.

Cheney, G. & Christensen, L. T. (2001) Organizational identity: Linkages between 'internal' and 'external' organizational communication. In Jablin, F. & Putnam, L. (eds.) *The New Handbook of Organizational Communication*. Sage Publications, Thousand Oaks, CA, pp. 231–269.

Cheney, G., Christensen, L. T. & Dailey, S. L. (2014) Communicating identity and identification in and around organizations. In Putnam, L. L. & Mumby, D. K. (eds.) *The Sage Handbook of Organizational Communication*. Sage Publications, Thousand Oaks, CA, pp. 695–716.

Cheney, G. & Cloud, D. L. (2006) Doing democracy, engaging the material employee participation and labor activity in an age of market globalization. *Management Communication Quarterly* 19, 501–540.

Cheney, G. & Tompkins, P. K. (1987) Coming to terms with organizational identification and commitment. *Central States Speech Journal* 38, 1–15.

Clair, R. P. (1996) The political nature of the colloquialism, "a real job": Implications for organizational socialization. *Communication Monographs* 66, 374–381.

Cloud, D. L. (1996) Hegemony or concordance? The rhetoric of tokenism in "Oprah" Oprah rags-to-riches biography. *Critical Studies in Media Communication* 13, 115–137.

Cloud, D. L. (2001) Laboring under the sign of the new. *Management Communication Quarterly* 15, 268–278.

Cloud, D. L. (2005) Fighting words: Labor and the limits of communication at Staley, 1993 to 1996. *Management Communication Quarterly* 18, 509–542.

Collins, B., Gill, R. & Mease, J. (2012) Exploring tensions in workplace relationships: Toward a communicative and situated understanding of Tokenism. In

References

Harden Fritz, J. M. & B. L. Omdahl (eds.) *Problematic Relationships in the Workplace, Volume II*. New York, NY: Peter Lang, pp. 193–213.

Collins, P. H. (1998) *Fighting Words: Black Women and The Search For Justice*. University of Minnesota Press, Minneapolis, MN.

Collinson, D. L. (1988) 'Engineering humour': Masculinity, joking and conflict in shop-floor relations. *Organization Studies* 9, 181–199.

Collinson, D. L. (2003) Identities and insecurities: Selves at work. *Organization* 10, 527–547.

Coombs, R., Knights, D. & Willmott, H. C. (1992) Culture, control and competition: Towards a conceptual framework for the study of information technology in organizations. *Organization Studies* 13, 51–72.

Cooren, F. (2004) Textual agency: How texts do things in organizational settings. *Organization* 11, 373–393.

Cooren, F. (2015) *Organizational Discourse: Communication and Constitution*. Polity Press, Cambridge, UK.

Corman, S. R. (2005) Postpositivism. In May, S. & Mumby, D. K. (eds.) *Engaging Organizational Communication Theory and Research: Multiple Perspectives*. Sage Publications, Thousand Oaks, CA, pp. 15–34.

Costas, J. & Grey, C. (2014) The power of temporality and the temporality of power: Imaginary future selves in professional service firms. *Organization Studies* 35, 909–937.

Costas, J. & Fleming, P. (2009) Beyond dis-identification: A discursive approach to self-alienation in contemporary organizations. *Human Relations* 62, 353–378.

Costas, J. & Kärreman, D. (2016) The bored self in knowledge work. *Human Relations* 69, 61–83.

Covey, S. R. (1989) *Seven Habits of Highly Effective People: Powerful Lessons in Personal Change*. Simon and Schuster, New York.

Craig, R. T. & Tracy, K. (1995) Grounded practical theory: The case of intellectual discussion. *Communication Theory* 5, 248–272.

Crenshaw, K. W. (1991) Mapping the margins: Intersectionality, identity politics, and violence against women of color. *Stanford Law Review* 46, 1241–1299.

Czarniawska-Joerges, B. (1994) Narratives of individual and organizational identities. In Deetz, S. (ed.) *Communication Yearbook* 17, Lawrence Erlbaum, Mahwah, NJ, pp. 193–221.

Daft, R. L. & Lengel, R. H. (1984) Information richness: A new approach to managerial behavior and organization design. In Staw, B. M. & Cummings, L. L. (eds.) *Research in Organizational Behavior Vol. 6*. JAI: Greenwich, CT, pp. 191–233.

Daft, R. L. & Lengel, R. H. (1986) Organizational information requirements, media richness and structural design. *Management Science* 32, 554–571.

Deal, T. E. & Kennedy, A. A. (1988) *Corporate Cultures: The Rites and Rituals of Corporate Life*. Penguin, New York.

Dean, M., Gill, R. & Barbour, J. B. (2016) "Let's sit forward": The successful (re)design of communication depends on understanding gendered occupational images and spatial and temporal materiality. *Health Communication* 31, 1506–1516.

Deetz, S. (1992) *Democracy in an Age of Corporate Colonization: Developments in Communication and The Politics of Everyday Life.* SUNY Press, Albany, NY.

Deetz, S. (1995) *Transforming Communication, Transforming Business: Building Responsive and Responsible Workplaces.* Hampton Press, Cresskill, NJ.

Deetz, S. (1996) Describing differences in approaches to organization science: Rethinking Burrell and Morgan and their legacy. *Organization Science* 7, 191–207.

Deetz, S. (1998) Discursive formations, strategized subordination, and self-surveillance: An empirical case. In McKinlay, A. & Starkey, K. (eds.) *Foucault, Management and Organization Theory.* Sage Publications, London, pp. 151–172.

Derrida, J. (1976) *Of Grammatology.* Trans. Spivak, G. Johns Hopkins University, Baltimore.

DiSanza, J. R. & Bullis, C. (1999) Everybody identifies with Smokey the Bear: Employee responses to newsletter identification inducements at the US Forest Service. *Management Communication Quarterly* 12, 347–399.

Discenna, T. A. (2010) The rhetoric of graduate employee unionization: Critical rhetoric and the Yale Grade Strike. *Communication Quarterly* 58, 19–35.

Down, S. & Reveley, J. (2009) Between narration and interaction: Situating first-line supervisor identity work. *Human Relations* 62, 379–401.

Drucker, P. (1994) The age of social transformation. *The Atlantic Monthly*, November, 274 (5), 53–80.

du Gay, P. (2004) Against 'Enterprise' (but not against 'enterprise', for that would make no sense). *Organization* 11, 37–57.

du Gay, P. & Salaman, G. (1992) The cult[ure] of the customer. *Journal of Management Studies* 29, 615–633.

Dukerich, J. M., Golden, B. R. & Shortell, S. M. (2002) Beauty is in the eye of the beholder: The impact of organizational identification, identity, and image on the cooperative behaviors of physicians. *Administrative Science Quarterly* 47, 507–533.

Edwards, D. (2011) *I'm Feeling Lucky: The Confessions of Google Employee Number 59.* Houghton Mifflin Harcourt, New York.

Edwards, R. (1979) *Contested Terrain: The Transformation of the Workplace in the Twentieth Century.* Basic Books, New York.

Ehrenreich, B. & Hochschild, A. R. (2003) *Global Woman: Nannies, Maids, and Sex Workers in the New Economy.* Metropolitan Books, New York.

Eleff, L. R. & Trethewey, A. (2006) The enterprising parent: A critical examination of parenting, consumption and identity. *Journal of the Motherhood Initiative for Research and Community Involvement* 8, 242–251.

Elsbach, K. D. & Bhattacharya, C.B. (2001) Defining who you are by what you're not: Organizational disidentification and the National Rifle Association. *Organization Science* 12, 393–413.

Essers, C. & Benschop, Y. (2007) Enterprising identities: Female entrepreneurs of Moroccan or Turkish origin in the Netherlands. *Organization Studies* 28, 49–69.

Essers, C. & Benshop, Y. (2008) Muslim businesswomen doing boundary work: The negotiation of Islam, gender and ethnicity within entrepreneurial contexts. *Human Relations* 62, 403–423.

Fairhurst, G. T. (2007) *Discursive Leadership: In Conversation with Leadership Psychology*. Sage Publications, Thousand Oaks, CA.

Fairhurst, G. T. & Putnam, L. (2004) Organizations as discursive constructions. *Communication Theory* 14, 5–26.

Ferguson, K. (1984) *The Feminist Case Against Bureaucracy*. Temple University Press: Philadelphia.

Fiol, C. M. (2002) Capitalizing on Paradox: The Role of Language in Transforming Organizational Identities. *Organization Science* 13, 653–666.

Florida, R. (2002) *The Rise of the Creative Class: And How It's Transforming Work, Leisure, Community and Everyday Life*. Basic Books, New York.

Florida, R. (2008) *Who's Your City? How the Creative Economy is Making Where You Live the Most Important Decision of Your Life*. Basic Books, New York.

Foucault, M. (1977a) *Discipline and Punish: The Birth of the Prison*. London, Penguin.

Foucault, M. (1997b) *Discipline and Punish: The Birth of the Prison*, 2nd edn. Trans. Sheridan, A. Vintage, New York.

Gagnon, S. (2008) Compelling identity: Selves and insecurity in global, corporate management development. *Management Learning* 39, 375–391.

Gailliard, B. M., Myers, K. K. & Seibold, D. R. (2010) Organizational assimilation: A multidimensional reconceptualization and measure. *Management Communication Quarterly* 24, 552–578.

Gamble, V. N. (2000) Subcutaneous scars. *Health Affairs* 19, 164–169.

Ganesh, S., Zoller, H. & Cheney, G. (2005) Transforming resistance, broadening our boundaries: Critical organizational communication meets globalization from below. *Communication Monographs* 72, 169–191.

Gardner, W. L., Avolio, B. J., Luthans, F., May, D. R. & Walumbwa, F. (2005) "Can you see the real me?" A self-based model of authentic leader and follower development. *The Leadership Quarterly* 16, 343–372.

Giddens, A. (1984) *The Constitution of Society*. University of California Press, Berkeley, CA.

References

Giddens, A. (1991) *Modernity and Self-Identity: Self and Society in the Late Modern Age.* Stanford University Press, Stanford, CA.

Gieryn, T. F. (2000) A space for place in sociology. *Annual Review of Sociology* 26, 463–496.

Gill, R. (2011) The shadow in organizational ethnography: Moving beyond shadowing to spect-acting. *Qualitative Research in Organizations and Management* 6, 115–133.

Gill, R. (2013) The evolution of organizational archetypes: From the American to the entrepreneurial dream. *Communication Monographs* 80, 331–353.

Gill, R. (2014) "If you're struggling to survive day-to-day": Class as optimism and contradiction in entrepreneurial discourse. *Organization* 21, 50–67.

Gill, R. & Barbour, J. B. (2016) The paradox of the lone wolf: Entrepreneur identity as collective-associative. Paper presented at the annual meeting of the National Communication Association, 10–13 November 2016. Philadelphia, Pennsylvania.

Gill, R. & Larson, G. S. (2014) Making the ideal (local) entrepreneur: Place and the regional development of high-tech entrepreneurial identity. *Human Relations* 67, 519–542.

Godwyn, M. (2009) Can the liberal arts and entrepreneurship work together? *American Association of University Professors (AAUP)* [online], January–February 2009. Available from: http://www.aaup.org/article/can-liberal-arts-and-entrepreneurship-work-together#.VxlBgyN96iY.

Gossett, L. M. & Kilker, J. (2006) My job sucks: Examining counterinstitutional web sites as locations for organizational member voice, dissent, and resistance. *Management Communication Quarterly* 20, 63–90.

Grant, D., Hardy, C., Oswick, C. & Putnam, L. L. (eds.) (2004) *The Sage Handbook of Organizational Discourse.* Sage Publications: London.

Halford, S. & Leonard, P. (2006) *Negotiating Gender Identities at Work: Place, Space, and Time.* New York, NY: Palgrave MacMillan.

Harquail, C. V. (1998) Organizational identification and the "whole person": Integrating affect, behavior, and cognition. In Whetten, D. A. & Godfrey, P. C. (eds.) *Identity in Organizations: Building Theory Through Conversations.* Sage Publications, Thousand Oaks, CA, pp. 223–231.

Harvey, D. (2005) *A Brief History of Neoliberalism.* Oxford University Press, New York.

Hochschild, A. R. (1983) *The Managed Heart: Commercialization of Human Feelings.* University of California Press, Berkeley, CA.

Hochschild, A. R. (1997) *The Time Bind: When Work Becomes Home and Home Becomes Work.* Henry Holt and Company, New York.

Hogg, M. A. & Terry, D. J. (2000) Social identity and self-categorization processes in organizational contexts. *Academy of Management Review* 25, 121–140.

References

Holmer Nadesan, M. (1996) Organizational identity and space of action. *Organization Studies* 17, 49–81.

Holmer Nadesan, M (2001) *Fortune* on globalization and the new economy. *Management Communication Quarterly* 14, 498–506.

Holmer Nadesan, M. & Trethewey, A. (2000) Performing the enterprising subject: Gendered strategies for success (?). *Text and Performance Quarterly* 20, 223–250.

Holstein, J. A. & Gubrium, J. F. (2000) *The Self We Live By: Narrative Identity in a Postmodern World*. Oxford University Press: New York.

Horkheimer, J. M. & Adorno, T. (1988) *Dialectic of Enlightenment*. Trans. Cumming, J. Continuum: New York.

Ibarra, H. (1999) Provisional selves: Experimenting with image and identity in professional adaptation. *Administrative Science Quarterly* 44, 764–791.

Ibarra, H. & Barbulescu, R. (2010) Identity as narrative: Prevalence, effectiveness, and consequences of narrative identity work in macro work role transitions. *Academy of Management Review* 35, 135–154.

Jablin, F. M. (2001) Organizational entry, assimilation and disengagement/exit. In Jablin, F. M. & Putnam, L. L. (eds.) *The New Handbook of Organizational Communication: Advances in Theory, Research, and Methods*. Sage Publications, Thousand Oaks, CA, pp. 732–818.

Jackson, M. H., Poole, M. S. & Kuhn, T. (2002) The social construction of technology in studies of the workplace. In Lievrouw, L. A. & Livingstone, S. (eds.) *Handbook of New Media: Social Shaping and Consequences of ICTs*. Sage Publications, London, pp. 236–253.

Jacques, R. (1996) *Manufacturing the Employee: Management Knowledge From the 19th to 21st Centuries*. Sage Publications, London.

James, E. P. & Gill, R. (2015) Developing and demonstrating the gendered capacity to (re)act in "xtreme" fitness programs. Paper accepted for presentation at the annual meeting of the International Communication Association, 21–25 May 2015. San Juan, Puerto Rico.

Jian, G. (2008) Identity and technology: Organizational control of knowledge-intensive work. *Qualitative Research Reports in Communication* 9, 62–71.

Jorgenson, J. (2002) Engineering selves: Negotiating gender and identity in technical work. *Management Communication Quarterly* 15, 350–380.

Kärreman, D. & Alvesson, M. (2009) Resisting resistance: Counter-resistance, consent and compliance in a consultancy firm. *Human Relations* 62, 1115–1144.

Kaufman, H. (1960) *The Forest Ranger: A Study in Administrative Behavior*. Johns Hopkins University Press: Baltimore, MD.

Kendall, B. E., Gill, R. & Cheney, G. (2007) Consumer activism and corporate social responsibility: How strong a connection. In Cheney, G., May, S. & Roper, J. (eds.) *The Debate Over Corporate Social Responsibility*. Oxford University Press, New York, pp. 241–264.

References

Kirby, E. L., Golden, A. G., Medved, C. E., Jorgenson, J. & Buzzanell, P. M. (2003) An organizational communication challenge to the discourse of work and family research: From problematics to empowerment. In Kalbfleisch, P. (ed.) *Communication Yearbook 27*, Lawrence Erlbaum, Mahwah, NJ, pp. 1–44.

Knight, G. (2007) Activism, risk, and communicational politics: Nike and the sweat-shop problem. In May, S., Cheney, G. & Roper, J. (eds.) *The Debate Over Corporate Social Responsibility*. Oxford University Press, New York, pp. 305–318.

Kondo, D. K. (1990) Crafting Selves: Power, Gender, and Discourses of Identity in a Japanese Workplace. University of Chicago Press, Chicago, IL.

Kramer, M. W. (2010) *Organizational Socialization: Joining and Leaving Organizations*. Polity Press, Cambridge, UK.

Kreiner, G. E., Hollensbe, E., Sheep, M. L., Smith, B. R. & Kataria, N. (2015) Elasticity and the dialectic tensions of organizational identity: How can we hold together while we are pulling apart? *Academy of Management Journal* 58, 981–1011.

Kuhn, T. (2006) A 'demented work ethic' and a 'lifestyle firm': Discourse, identity, and workplace time commitments. *Organization Studies*, 27, 1339–1358.

Kuhn, T. (2009) Positioning lawyers: Discursive resources, professional ethics and identification. *Organization* 16, 681–704.

Kuhn, T. & Nelson, N. (2002) Reengineering identity: A case study of multiplicity and duality in organizational identification. *Management Communication Quarterly* 16, 5–38.

Kunda, G. (1992) *Engineering Culture: Control and Commitment in a High-Tech Organization*. Temple University Press, Philadelphia.

Lair, D. J. & Wieland, S. M. B. (2012) "What are you going to do with that major?": Colloquial speech and the meanings of work and education. *Management Communication Quarterly* 26, 423–452.

Larson, G. S. & Pearson, A. R. (2012) Placing identity: Place as a discursive resource for occupational identity work among high-tech entrepreneurs. *Management Communication Quarterly* 26, 241–266.

Larson, G. S. & Pepper, G. L. (2003) Strategies for managing multiple organizational identifications: A case of competing identities. *Management Communication Quarterly* 16, 528–557.

Larson, G. S. & Tompkins, P. K. (2005) Ambivalence and resistance: A study of management in a concertive control system. *Communication Monographs* 72, 1–21.

Leonardi, P. M. (2012) *Car Crashes without Cars: Lessons about Simulation Technology and Organizational Change from Automotive Design*. MIT Press, Cambridge, MA.

Limerick, P. N. (1987) *The Legacy of Conquest: The Unbroken Past of the American West*. W. W. Norton: New York.

References

Lindlof, T. R. & Taylor, B. C. (2011) *Qualitative Communication Research Methods*, 3rd edn. Sage Publications, Thousand Oaks, CA.

Lohr, S. (2015) IBM creates Watson health to analyze medical data. *The New York Times* Bits Blog [online], 13 April 2015. Available from: http://bits.blogs.nytimes.com/2015/04/13/ibm-creates-watson-health-to-analyze-medical-data/?_r=0.

Lord, R. G. & Brown, D. J. (2004) *Leadership Processes and Follower Self-Identity*. Lawrence Elrbaum, Mahwah, NJ.

Lutgen-Sandvik, P. (2008) Intensive remedial identity work: Responses to workplace bullying trauma and stigmatization. *Organization* 15, 97–119.

Mael, F. A. & Ashforth, B. E. (1992) Alumni and their alma mater: A partial test of the reformulated model of organizational identification. *Journal of Organizational Behavior* 13, 103–123.

Mael, F. A. & Ashforth, B. E. (1995) Loyal from day one: Biodata, organizational identification, and turnover among newcomers. *Personnel Psychology* 48, 309–333.

Markus, H. & Nurius, P. (1986) Possible selves. *American Psychologist* 41, 954–969.

Mastroianni, B. (2014) IBM's Watson helps Mayo Clinic match cancer patients with clinical trials. *FoxNews.com* [online], 11 September 2014. Available from: http://www.foxnews.com/tech/2014/09/11/ibms-watson-heads-to-mayo-clinic-to-match-cancer-patients-with-clinical-trials.html.

May, S. & Mumby, D. K. (eds.) (2005) *Engaging Organizational Communication Theory and Research: Multiple Perspectives*. Sage Publications, Thousand Oaks, CA.

McCall, L. (2005) The complexity of intersectionality. *Signs: Journal of Women in Culture and Society* 30, 1771–1800.

McDonald, J. (2015) Organizational communication meets queer theory: Theorizing relations of "difference" differently. *Communication Theory* 25, 310–329.

McKerrow, R. E. (1989) Critical rhetoric: Theory and praxis. *Communications Monographs* 56, 91–111.

McMillan, J. J. & Cheney, G. (1996) The student as consumer: The implications and limitations of a metaphor. *Communication Education* 45, 1–15.

Medved, C. E. & Kirby, E. L. (2005) Family CEOs: A feminist analysis of corporate mothering discourses. *Management Communication Quarterly* 18, 435–478.

Meisenbach, R. J. (2008) Working with tensions: Materiality, discourse, and (dis)empowerment in occupational identity negotiation among higher education fundraisers. *Management Communication Quarterly* 22, 258–287.

Meriläinen, S., Tienari, J., Thomas, R. & Davies, A. (2004) Management consultant talk: A cross-cultural comparison of normalizing discourse and resistance. *Organization* 11, 539–564.

References

Miller, F. A. & French, M. (2016) Organizing the entrepreneurial hospital: Hybridizing the logics of healthcare and innovation. *Research Policy* 45, 1534–1544.

Miller, V., Allen, M., Casey, M. & Johnson, J. (2000) Reconsidering the organizational identification questionnaire. *Management Communication Quarterly* 13, 626–658.

Mowday, R. T., Steers, R. M. & Porter, L. W. (1979) The measurement of organizational commitment. *Journal of Vocational Behavior* 14, 224–247.

Mumby, D. K. (1997) The problem of hegemony: Rereading Gramsci for organizational communication studies. *Western Journal of Communication* 61, 343–375.

Mumby, D. K. (2000) Common ground from the critical perspective: Overcoming binary oppositions. In Corman, S. R. & Poole, M. S. (eds.) *Perspectives on Organizational Communication: Finding Common Ground*. The Guilford Press, New York, pp. 68–86.

Mumby, D. K. (2005) Theorizing resistance in organization studies: A dialectical approach. *Management Communication Quarterly* 19, 19–44.

Mumby, D. K. (2011) What's cooking in organizational discourse studies? A response to Alvesson and Kärreman. *Human Relations* 64, 1147–1161.

Mumby, D. K. (2013) *Organizational Communication: A Critical Approach.* Sage Publications: Thousand Oaks, CA.

Murphy, A. G. (1998) Hidden transcripts of flight attendant resistance. *Management Communication Quarterly* 11, 499–535.

Musson, G. & Duberly, J. (2007) Change, change or be exchanged: The discourse of participation and the manufacture of identity. *Journal of Management Studies* 44, 143–164.

Nash, J. C. (2008) Re-thinking intersectionality. *Feminist Review* 89, 1–15.

Nelson, A. J. & Irwin, J. (2014) "Defining what we do – all over again": Occupational identity, technological change, and the librarian/internet-search relationship. *Academy of Management Journal* 57, 892–928.

Nippert-Eng, C. E. (1996) *Home and Work: Negotiating Boundaries Through Everyday Life*. University of Chicago Press, Chicago, IL.

Novak, D. R. (2010) Democratizing qualitative research: Photovoice and the study of human communication. *Communication Methods and Measures* 4, 291–310.

Nyberg, D. & Sveningsson, S. (2014) Paradoxes of authentic leadership: Leader identity struggles. *Leadership* 10, 437–455.

Parker, P. S. (2005) *Race, Gender, and Leadership: Re-Envisioning Organizational Leadership from the Perspectives of African American Women Executives*. Lawrence Erlbaum Associates, Mahwah, New Jersey.

Parker, P. S. (2014) Difference and organizing. In Putnam, L. L. & Mumby, D. K. (eds.) *The SAGE Handbook of Organizational Communication: Advances in Theory, Research, and Methods*. Sage Publications, Thousand Oaks, CA, pp. 619–643.

References

Pepper, G. L. & Larson, G. S. (2006) Cultural identity tensions in a post-acquisition organization. *Journal of Applied Communication Research* 34, 49–71.

Peters, T. & Waterman, R. (1982) *In Search of Excellence: Lessons from America's Best-Run Corporations*. Warner, New York.

Postmes, T., Spears, R. & Lea, M. (1998) Breaching or building social boundaries? SIDE-effects of computer-mediated communication. *Communication Research* 25, 689–715.

Postmes, T., Spears, R. & Lea, M. (2000) The formation of group norms in computer-mediated communication. *Human Communication Research* 26, 341–371.

Pratt, M. G. (2001) Social identity dynamics in modern organizations: An organizational psychology=organizational behavior perspective. In Hogg, M. A. & Terry, D. J. (eds.) *Social Identity Processes in Organizational Contexts*. Psychology Press, Philadelphia, PA, pp. 13–30.

Pringle, R. (1989) *Secretaries Talk: Sexuality, Power And Work*. Verso, London.

Putnam, L. L. (2015) Unpacking the dialectic: Alternative views on the discourse-materiality relationship. *Journal of Management Studies* 52, 706–716.

Putnam, L. L. & Nicotera, A. M. (2009) *Building Theories of Organization: The Constitutive Role of Communication*. Routledge, London.

Putnam, L. L. & Pacanowsky, M. E. (1983) *Communication and Organizations: An Interpretive Approach*. Sage Publications, Thousand Oaks, CA.

Riketta, M. (2005) Organizational identification: A meta-analysis. *Journal of Vocational Behavior* 66, 358–384.

Rock, K. W. & Pratt, M. G. (2002) Where do we go from here? Predicting identification among dispersed employees. In Moingeon, B. & Soenen, G. (eds.) *Corporate and Organizational Identities: Integrating Strategy, Marketing, Communication, and Organizational Perspectives*. Routledge, London, pp. 51–71.

Rose, N. (1998) *Inventing ourselves: Psychology, power and personhood*. Cambridge University Press, Cambridge, UK.

Rotham, J. (2016) Shut up and sit down: Why the leadership industry rules. *The New Yorker*, 29 February 2016.

Russo, T. C. (1998) Organizational and professional identification: A case of newspaper journalists. *Management Communication Quarterly* 12, 72–111.

Salazar Parrenas, R. (2001) *Servants of Globalization: Women, Migration, and Domestic Work*. Stanford University Press, Stanford, CA.

Sass, J. S. & Canary, D. J. (1991) Organizational commitment and identification: An examination of conceptual and operational convergence. *Western Journal of Speech Communication* 55, 275–293.

Schwarze, S. (2003) Corporate-state irresponsiblity, critical publicity, and asbestos exposure in Libby, Montana. *Management Communication Quarterly* 16, 625.

Scott, C. R. (1997) Identification with multiple targets in a geographically dispersed organization. *Management Communication Quarterly* 10, 491–522.

Scott, C. R. (1999) The impact of physical and discursive anonymity on group members' multiple identifications during computer-supported decision making. *Western Journal of Communication (includes Communication Reports)* 63, 456–487.

Scott, C. R. (2007) Communication and Social Identity Theory: Existing and potential connections in organizational identification research. *Communication Studies* 58, 123–138.

Scott, C. R., Connaughton, S. L., Diaz-Saenz, H., Maguire, K., Ramirez, R., Richardson, B., Shaw, S. P. & Morgan, D. (1999) The impacts of communication and multiple identifications on intent to leave: A multi-methodological exploration. *Management Communication Quarterly* 12, 400–435.

Scott, C. R., Corman, S. R. & Cheney, G. (1998) Development of a structurational model of identification in the organization. *Communication Theory* 8, 298–336.

Scott, C. R. & Stephens, K. K. (2009) It depends on who you're talking to . . . : Predictors and outcomes of situated measures of organizational identification. *Western Journal of Communication* 72, 370–394.

Scott, C. R. & Timmerman, C. E. (1999) Communication technology use and multiple workplace identifications among organizational teleworkers with varied degrees of virtuality. *IEEE Transactions of Professional Communication* 42, 240–260.

Searle, J. R. (1985) *Expression and Meaning: Studies in the Theory of Speech Acts*. Cambridge University Press, London.

Selingo, J. J. (2014) Demystifying the MOOC. *The New York Times* [online], 29 October 2014. Available from: http://www.nytimes.com/2014/11/02/education/edlife/demystifying-the-mooc.html.

Sewell, G. (1998) The discipline of teams: The control of team-based industrial work through electronic and peer surveillance. *Administrative Science Quarterly* 43, 397–428.

Shortt, H. (2012) Identityscapes of a hair salon: Work identities and the value of visual methods. *Sociological Research Online* 17, 22. Available from: http://www.socresonline.org.uk/17/2/22.html.

Shortt, H. & Warren, S. (2012) Fringe benefits: valuing the visual in narratives of hairdressers' identities at work. *Visual Studies* 27, 18–34.

Sigman, S. J. (1995) *The Consequentiality of Communication*. Psychology Press, New York.

Simon, H. A. (1976) *Administrative Behavior*, 3rd edn. Free Press, New York.

Sitkin, S. B., Sutcliffe, K. M. & Barrios-Choplin, J. R. (1992) A dual-capacity model of communication media choice in organizations. *Human Communication Research* 18, 563–598.

Slutskaya, N., Simpson, A. & Hughes, J. (2012) Lessons from photoelicitation:

References

Encouraging working men to speak. *Qualitative Research in Organizations and Management: An International Journal* 7, 16–33.

Smith, R. C. & Eisenberg, E. M. (1987) Conflict at Disneyland: A root-metaphor analysis. *Communications Monographs* 54, 367–380.

Sohrabi, B., Gholipour, A. & Amiri, B. (2012) The influence of information technology on organizational behavior: Study of identity challenges. In Information Resources Management Association (eds.) *Human Resources Management: Concepts, Methodologies, Tools, and Applications, Vol 1*. Information Science Reference, Hershey, PA, pp. 23–39.

Sveningsson, S. & Alvesson, M. (2003) Managing managerial identities: Organizational fragmentation, discourse and identity struggle. *Human Relations* 56, 1163–1193.

Symon, G. (2008) Developing the political perspective on technological change through rhetorical analysis. *Management Communication Quarterly* 22, 74–98.

Tajfel, H. & Turner, J. C. (1986) The social identity theory of intergroup behavior. In Worchel, S. & Austin, W. G. (eds.) *Psychology of Intergroup Relations*, 2nd ed. Nelson-Hall, Chicago, pp. 7–24.

Taylor, B. (2005) Postmodern Theory. In May, S. & Mumby, D. K. (eds.) *Engaging Organizational Communication Theory and Research: Multiple Perspectives*. Sage Publications, Thousand Oaks, CA, pp. 113–140.

Taylor, J. R. & Van Every, E. (2000) *The Emergent Organization: Communication at Its Site and Surface*. Lawrence Erlbaum, Mahwah, NJ.

Thatcher, S. & Zhu, X. (2006) Changing identities in a changing workplace: Identification, identity enactment, self-verification, and telecommuting. *Academy of Management Review* 31, 1076–1088.

The Editors (2015) New directions in studying discourse and materiality. *Journal of Management Studies* 52, 678–679.

Thornborrow, T. & Brown, A.D. (2009) 'Being regimented': Aspiration, discipline and identity work in the British parachute regiment. *Organization Studies* 30, 355–376.

Tompkins, P. K. (1993) *Organizational Communication Imperatives: Lessons of the Space Program*. Roxbury, Los Angeles.

Tompkins, P. K. (2005) *Apollo, Challenger, Columbia: The Decline of the Space Program: A Study in Organizational Communication*. Roxbury Publishing Co., Los Angeles.

Tompkins, P. K. (2009) *Who Is My Neighbor?: Communicating and Organizing to End Homelessness*. Paradigm Publishers, Boulder CO.

Tompkins, P. K. & Cheney, G. (1983) Account analysis of organizations: Decision-making and identification. In Putnam, L. L. & Pacanowsky, M. (eds.) *Communication and Organizations: An Interpretive Approach*. Sage Publications, Beverly Hills, CA, pp. 123–146.

Tompkins, P. K. & Cheney, G. (1985) Communication and unobtrusive control in contemporary organizations. In McPhee, R. & Tompkins. P. K. (eds.) *Organizational Communication: Traditional Themes and New Directions.* Sage Publications, Newbury Park, CA, pp. 179–210.

Townley, B. (1993) Foucault, power/knowledge, and its relevance for human resource management. *Academy of Management Review* 18, 518–545.

Townsend, A. (2014) Cleveland Clinic-IBM Watson collaboration highlighted at medical innovation summit. *The Plains Dealer, Cleveland.com* [online] 29 October 2014. Available from: http://www.cleveland.com/healthfit/index. ssf/2014/10/cleveland_clinic-ibm_watson_collaboration_highlighted_at_medi cal_innovation_summit.html.

Toyoki, S. & Brown, A. D. (2013) Stigma, identity and power: Managing stigmatized identities through discourse. *Human Relations* 67, 715–737.

Tracy, S. J. (2000) Becoming a character for commerce emotion labor, self-subordination, and discursive construction of identity in a total institution. *Management Communication Quarterly* 14, 90–128.

Tracy, S. J. (2013) *Qualitative Research Methods: Collecting Evidence, Crafting Analysis, Communicating Impact.* Malden, MA: Wiley Blackwell.

Tracy, S. J. & Trethewey, A. (2005) Fracturing the real-self↔fake-self dichotomy: Moving toward "crystallized" organizational discourses and identities. *Communication Theory* 15, 168–195.

Trethewey, A. (1997) Resistance, identity, and empowerment: A postmodern feminist analysis of clients in a human service organization. *Communication Monographs* 64, 281–301.

Trethewey, A. (1999) Disciplined bodies: Women's embodied identities at work. *Organization Studies* 20, 423–450.

Trethewey, A. (2001) Reproducing and resisting the master narrative of decline: Midlife professional women's experiences of aging. *Management Communication Quarterly* 15, 183–226.

Trethewey, A. & Ashcraft, K. L. (2004) Special issue introduction. Practicing disorganization: The development of applied perspectives on living with tension. *Journal of Applied Communication Research* 32, 81–88.

Turner, P. K. & Norwood, K. (2013) Unbounded motherhood: Embodying a good working mother identity. *Management Communication Quarterly* 27, 396–424.

Urciuoli, B. (2014) The semiotic production of the good student: A Piercean look at the commodification of liberal arts education. *Signs and Society* 2, 56–83.

Van Maanen, J. (2006) Ethnography then and now. *Qualitative Research in Organizations and Management: An International Journal* 1, 13–21.

Waldman, P. (2010) The oddly unpopular estate tax. *The American Prospect* [online], 16 December 2010. Available from: http://prospect.org/article/oddly-unpopular-estate-tax.

Wallis, D. (2012) Komen foundation struggles to regain wide support. *The New York Times*, 9 November 2012, p. F2.

References

Walther, J. B. & Parks, M. R. (2002) Cues filtered out, cues filtered in. In Knapp, M. L. & Daly, J. A. (eds.) *Handbook of Interpersonal Communication*. Sage Publications, Thousand Oaks, CA, pp. 529–563.

Wang, C. C. (1999) Photovoice: A participatory action research strategy applied to women's health. *Journal of Women's Health* 8, 185–192.

Wang, C. & Burris, M. A. (1994) Empowerment through photo novella: Portraits of participation. *Health Education Quarterly* 21, 171–186.

Watson, T. (2008) Managing identity, identity work, personal predicaments and structured circumstances. *Organization* 15, 121–143.

Watson, T. J. (2009) Narrative, life story and manager identity: A case study in autobiographical identity work. *Human Relations* 62, 425–452.

Weick, K. E. (1995) *Sensemaking in Organizations*. Sage Publications, Thousand Oaks, CA.

Weissmann, J. (2013) Here's exactly how many college graduates live back at home. *The Atlantic Monthly* [online], 26 February 2013. Available from: http://www.theatlantic.com/business/archive/2013/02/heres-exactly-how-many-college-graduates-live-back-at-home/273529/.

Wells, C. (2013) Controlling "good science": Language, national identity, and occupational control in scientific work. *Management Communication Quarterly* 27, 319–345.

Wells, C., Gill, R. & McDonald, J. (2015) "Us foreigners": Intersectionality in a scientific organization. *Equality, Diversity and Inclusion: An International Journal* 34, 539–553.

West, C. & Fenstermaker, S. (1995) Doing difference. *Gender & Society* 9, 8–37.

Wetherell, M., Taylor, S. & Yates, S. J. (2001) *Discourse as Data: A Guide for Analysis*. Sage Publications, London.

White, G. B. (2016) Is a different kind of Silicon Valley possible? *The Atlantic Monthly* [online], 24 March 2016. Available from: www.theatlantic.co,/business/archive/2016/03/ duham-startup-entrepreneurship/475269.

Wickman, C. (2014) Rhetorical framing in corporate press releases: The case of British Petroleum and the Gulf oil spill. *Environmental Communication* 8, 3–20.

Wieland, S. M. (2010) Ideal selves as resources for the situated practice of identity. *Management Communication Quarterly* 24, 503–528.

Williams, E. A. & Connaughton, S. L. (2012) Expressions of identifications: The nature of talk and identity tensions among organizational members in a struggling organization. *Communication Studies* 63, 457–481.

Willis, P. E. (1977) *Learning To Labor: How Working Class Kids Get Working Class Jobs*. Columbia University Press Morningside Edition, Columbia, NY.

Witz, A. & Savage, M. (1992) The gender of organizations. In Savage, M. & Witz, A. (eds.) *Gender and Bureaucracy*. Blackwell/The Sociological Review, Oxford, UK, pp. 3–64.

References

Woodstock, L. (2014) Tattoo therapy: Storying the self on reality TV in neoliberal times. *The Journal of Popular Culture* 47, 780–799.

Ziemer, J. A. (2016) "Entrepreneurs of the church world": Investigating intersections between enterprise discourse and the occupational identity of church planters. Unpublished dissertation, Texas A&M University.

Zikic, J. & Richardson, J. (2015) What happens when you can't be who you are: Professional identity at the institutional periphery. *Human Relations* 69, 139–168.

Zoller, H. M. (2014) Power and resistance in organizational communication. In Putnam, L. L. & Mumby, D. K. (eds.) *The SAGE Handbook of Organizational Communication: Advances in Theory, Research, and Methods*, 3rd edn. Sage Publications, Thousand Oaks, CA, pp. 595–618.

Index

Index

Index

Index

organizational identity. *See* organizational identity
globalisation and, 3–5, 7
identity work. *See* identity work
insecurity, 47–50, 84, 86–94, 143
intersectionality, 68, 89–94, 152, 158
multiple identities, 4, 7–9, 137–138
real self↔fake self, 87–89, 137
regulation. *See* identity regulation
researching. *See* researching identity
social identity theory (SIT), 58–63
tensions, 72
work and. *See* work
identity consumption, 5
identity regulation
abuse, 168–169
broad discourses, 108–110
decision-making and, 147
discipline, 106–107
enterprise discourse, 109–110
Foucauldian approaches, 105–108
leadership and, 138–143
locale-specific discourses, 110–112
meaning, 74–75, 104
neoliberal discourse, 108–110
organizational cultures, 112–113
organizational practice, 167–168
organizational socialization of employees, 112–113
power, 105–106
producing, 104–114
resistance, 114–124
rhetoric, 113–14
self-subordination, 107–108
tensions, 72
identity work
crisis, instability and change, 73–4
definition, 63
discursive resources, 65–67, 71, 143–144
ideal selves, 71–72
identity regulation and, 40
identity tensions, 72

leadership and, 143–146
meaning, 4
narrating identities, 68–70
occupational identity, 67–68
overview, 63–74
possible selves, 70
preferred selves, 70–71
provisional selves, 71
space of action, 144
substance, 64–68
IGERT, 45–46
individualism, 2–3, 137, 156
information and communication technology. *See* technology
innovation ecosystems, 153–154
Internet, 79–80, 85, 128, 134
intersectional identities, 8–9, 27–28, 68, 89–94, 152, 158
interviews, 163–164
Irwin, J., 134

Jacques, R., 106
JAR, 96
Jian, G., 135–136
Jobs, Steve, 41, 55
Jorgenson, J., 65
Josserand, E., 151

Kärreman, D., 32, 119
Kaufman, H., 21, 54
Kennedy, A. A., 112
Kirby, E. L., 73
Knights, D., 133
knowledge workers, 104, 119, 134, 135–136
Kondo, D. K., 116
Kramer, Michael, 148–149
Kuhn, Tim, 9, 38, 57, 65, 111, 163
Kunda, Gideon, 66–67, 103, 112, 135

Lair, D. J., 73
language, human capital, 93
Larson, Gregory, 16–17, 82, 111–112, 120–121, 136, 153, 163–164

Index

Index

Index